Once Upon A Fiend

Noir
Publishing

PO Box 28
Hereford
HR1 1YT
email: noir@appleonline.net

Once Upon A Fiend
By Ratfink and Pete McKenna
ISBN 0 9536564 1 1
© Ratfink and Pete McKenna 2000, all rights reserved
First published 2000 by:
Noir Publishing
Copyright© Noir Publishing 2000
Photos taken from the private Rodent Collection
Please note:- this book is in no way an official Alien Sex Fiend publication

British Library Cataloguingi in Publication Data:
A catalogue record for this book is available from the British Library.

Acknowledgments

Eternal thanks from Pete McKenna to the following people for their love, enthusiasm, cynicism, humour and support over the years. To Queenie, Karen, Ged Grennell and family, Chris Hewitt and family, John Gosman, the pin-striped question mark, Steve Cooke who started the ball rolling back in Brixton during those riotous nights, and last but certainly not least, Lisa Moylett who somehow manages to keep the flame burning.

Pete McKenna is currently involved in several writing and screenplay projects; Who The Hell's Frank Wilson ? - a Get Carter meets Human Traffic story set around the northern soul scene in 70's Manchester. The German Architect - a cold, harrowing narrative of an unrepentant SS officer's role in the Holocaust. Sisters - a story of murder and retribution set amid the dark labyrinths of the sado masochistic scene, and A Brief Moment In Time - the highs and lows of an adolescent love affair between a teenage kid and his cherished Lambretta scooter in 70's Blackpool.

Ratfink wishes to thank Maureen Wilson, Walter Wilson, Steve "Wiz", Stewart, Brian "Renfield" Nelson, Paul, Angie, Zoe McVeigh, Andy 456, Swill, Paul Bainbridge (Benny), Moz from Leeds, Andy Roberts, Harvey Birrell, Jim Lusted, Wolfgang, John Boath, Herbie, Lew, Chryste Hall at Xena Media, Ted & Mary Alexander, Billy Young, Ross Bowman, Giz Vandeklevt & family (House in the Woods), Nicci & Paul, Simon Peacock, Phil Leatham, Cherry, The Young Godz (Franz), GBH, John Bentham, Richard King, Johnny Moran, Martin Mercer, the arch Fiends of course - Nik, Chris & Doc and finally Andy Black for making another dream come true.

Special thanks to Vincent Locke for the chapter page artwork & to Graham Humphries for the Hammer Films collage and original back cover artwork.

This book is dedicated to Kashia-Cherry Wilson

CONTENTS

INTRODUCTION

Approximately seven miles from the kiss me quick, rock sucking mayhem of big dipperville, lies the place where this story began. The quintessential English village of Lytham. A small exclusive chunk or real estate, representing to many people young and old, the ultimate panacea to justify a lifetime of toil and trouble. With it's picture postcard windmill on the green and quaint fishermans cottages, one simply has to say that when one has arrived in Lytham, one has arrived in life !

On the surface, a wealthy, conservative, tweed and twinset nirvana where lazy days are spent browsing for brogues in gentlemans outiftters and sampling the latest exotic cheeses and pates in the corner delicatessen. Where deaf, blind pensioners idle up the high street in pristine Jensen Interceptors, oblivious to anything connected to road safety : where failed tycoons take refuge in Mummy and Daddy's bosom ; licking their wounds while planning the next multi million pound campaign : where the mere sight of a smiling bobby reassures the locals that nothing nasty is ever going to disturb their leafy tranquillity.

But underneath the crusty middle class veneer, Lytham boasts a thriving alternative sex drugs rock an roll subculture. It can still be found there today if you know where to look, but back in the 70's and 80's, finding it wasn't a problem. The place was mental house parties here, there, everywhere with plenty of controlled substances to make sure you regretted every second of your binge up, the morning after.

Headquarters of the scene ; a seafront pub called The Queens, frequented by all the main faces on the local rock scene from which, many legends were born. Two in particular : The Turnpike Cruisers, fronted by the inimitable Richard " Queenie " King, who once performed a live set hanging from the rafters one crazy night , and the Buggs. Lytham's answer to the Clash ; a power packed band fronted by the one and only Russ Caskey.

Crazy characters one and all, working their arses off in bands, hoping to pull off the big one. And what about the ambitious young punk kid walking down the high street, dressed in top hat and tails, make up and dyed hair. His head crammed full of dreams of rock an roll stardom : helping old ladies across the road, as he strolled down to the post office to cash his giro, wondering if he was going to make it or not ?

This a story of a dream come true born during a freezing cold, big overcoat winter : one of countless conversations over lager and frothy coffee in the woodchipped, emulsioned crypt of crap that is to art and culture what the Belgrano was to state of the art weapons technology. The DHSS crack palace itself ; Blackpool !.

Dreams. . . dreams. . . dreams ! You name it we dream it. Sexy, outrageous, improbable, greedy. For some, the thrill of walking out onto the Old Trafford pitch alongside the likes of Beckham, Giggs, Cole and Yorke represents the ultimate buzz. The latest Man United talent eager to prove himself in front of the ever faithful Red army.

Simpler dreams of holidaying in exotic sun drenched locations. Filling your face full of chilled Bacardi as you lie belly up like some beached whale on a deserted expanse of white sand and crystal clear aquamarine water tickling your toes. Desperately trying to ignore the fact that in a weeks time, it's back to the terraced house , the freezing cold building site , Butlins for the next five years , and fish and chips on a Friday night as the memory of the Caribbean takes a bad second place to the buzz of the six fifteen early morning call. . . aarrggghhh shit !

Macho posing dreams of riding out on that gleaming black and chrome customised Harley that's been laughing at you everytime you crawl past the window with your tongue trailing on the pavement. Knowing you'll never afford it but still , the dream convinces you to stay cool ; stick a tenner a week away and in a couple of years ; well you might just be able to afford the handlebars !.

Quitting the nine to five treadmill dreams forever as the overweight pinstriped, chisel faced boss pulls you in the office for another ticking off over your abysmal timekeeping. " Yes Mr Hargreaves. No Mr Hargreaves and get this you fat fucker Mr Hargreaves " as he pushes you that bit further to the dream of stomping him into the executive shag pile carpet once and for all with a " fuck you Mr Hargreaves. I'm off " leaving him fumbling around for the broken specs you've just crunched into a zillion pieces.

Full on sex dreams of just how exquisite it would be to spend a weekend of unparalleled carnality with the ravishing brunette in the tight skirt, giving you the big smiling come on , as she suggestively caresses a cocktail cherry between her moist pouting red lips. The wife asks " Is everything alright dear ? ". You nod and smile : the dream dying quicker than your hard on as you twirl another fork full of spaghetti up into your mouth ; dutifully returning the eternal answer she longs to hear. " Of course it is dear. Why shouldn't it be ?. More wine ? ".

And then there are those crazy rock n roll dreams we've all had now and again. Standing in your bedroom in front of the mirror doing your best Status Quo air guitar number ; head crammed full of making it bigtime as a rock god. Shea Stadium : wild swimming pool sex , drugs , debauchery and worldwide critical acclaim as your first album blasts into top spot.

And there he is. The balding, podgy, pushing fifty, cocaine snorting local rock god, who can still pull a bird as he spellbinds them with lines of how fuckin' great he was and how it all went wrong. The one who tells you that it's all cool man : who is still getting the ultimate band together ; still sending off countless numbers of crappy, second division demo tapes in a last gasp attempt to pull off the big one before it all finally goes pear shaped.

" Don't worry man cause it's all sorted. Sussed and in the bag. A few more weeks and I'm outta' here " he tells you as he swallows his pint ; slithers to the stage in the basement club for zeros. Sits down cross legged on his stool : finishes off the last joint before asking the never ending question in a futile attempt to break up the mindnumbing nocturnal banality of jamming Beatles , Bob Dylan and Fleetwood Mac ditties.

" Any requests out there ? " he mumbles in his best laid back west coast north of Watford hippie voice. " Got any Sinatra ? " shouts a purple faced , drunken slaphead propped up against the bar of the dingy smoke filled subterranean hell. You laugh as local rock n roll hero casts you a look that says it all as he plink plinks his way through an acoustic version of My Way for the zillionth time.

" Regrets I've had a few ". That's one side of the rock n roll dream the majority of musos have to live with, but what about the other side of the coin. What about Andy Wilson's dream when he was the young punk rock drummer nervously waiting backstage at The Astoria ; seconds away from storming the stage with the band he dreamed of playing in ever since hearing their first tape. A packed home town gig in front of the intensely loyal army of fans waiting to see what the new beat boy looked and sounded like for the first time. A band whose music had influenced and touched him deeply throughout his formative years. Then to begin an eight year relationship with the band in which he experienced all the highs and lows of the rock n roll lifestyle.

A full on 3-d technicolour kaleidoscope in which he met his all time rock idol Alice Cooper ; gigged to packed audiences from Nottingham to Tokyo ; suffered the emotional trauma of his marriage disintegrating as a result of the pressures the lifestyle heaped upon him ; was nearly decapitated in a vicious somewhat ironic streetfight in Belgium, as well as facing numerous death threats during one of the bands successful tours in Germany.

That was back in eighty seven : the band, those homegrown, deadpan darlings of the UK Goth rock scene : early exponents of the death gore horror disco theatre experience ; Alien Sex Fiend. The decomposed, transvestite alter ego of that irrepressible, cheeky cockney crooner, Mr Nik Fiend.

The Goth scene is back bigtime. Enjoying a 90's resurgence in popularity with bands like Cradle Of Filth, Placebo, and that androgynous mutant devil rocker Marilyn Manson shocking audiences worldwide with his own particular brew of theatrical horror show, strongly reminiscent of the time Alice Cooper stalked the stage with his Baby Jane persona, setting the precedent for horror rock shows to come , before opting for the more genteel pursuit of golf.

But all things ; rock an roll dreams included , come to an end. So too, for this dreamer, who's story you are about to read as he recalls the emotional highs and lows of a crazy, unforgettable, roller coaster lifestyle that will live with him forever. One that began with a knock on the door, on a cold, snow filled night when the Bowman came calling.

CHAPTER ONE

Believe It Or not

You know that special vibe in life, that screams at you to go for it no matter what ? Well sometimes you gotta' follow that scream. Go for the jugular, as I did when Ross Bowman rang the doorbell. Jumped in the van and headed down to London to John Henry's rehearsal studios ; my emotions all over the place, wondering what lay ahead for me. The only thing I was sure of that night : it was time to turn my ultimate dream into reality. Playing the drums for Alien Sex Fiend.

Looking back to that crazy time in my life , I knew it could only have been Alien Sex Fiend for me. Sure, there were other bands that sent a tingle down my spine but I just knew Nik and I were from the same mould. Both suffused with identical influences and addictions : Punk , Alice Cooper , Texas Chainsaw Massacre , Cramps , Clockwork Orange, Football , Hammer Horror , Monty Python , Sex , Drugs and other naughty ingredients, that represent to many people, the very spice of life.

The Fiends abode in Brixton was the final destination of that bitterly cold all night nocturnal journey but there were other journeys going on in my head that night : particularly my sudden metamorphosis from Fiend fanclub member to fully participating band member , faced with the awesome task of living up to my newly christened alter ego Rat Fink. The latest addition to Nik Fiends crazy view of the big wide world.

My arrival in Brixton was celebrated with warm welcoming smiles and handshakes plus a hot cuppa tea and spliff to help thaw me out. The Fiendish couple owned a great flat covered with a profusion of artwork painted on the walls. Voodoo squiggles and lot's of boneyard stuff but that was Nik for you. Very much into his art. I kipped down on the couch gradually recovering from the journey while at the same time, feeling slightly hesitant at what lay ahead for me drums wise. John Henry's was the top place to rehearse in : that first night I was in at the deep end as we kicked off with some classic Fiend tunes to spice up the atmosphere. Ignore The Machine , RIP , Dead and Buried , Boneshaker Baby plus some stuff new to my ears Nik had been working on.

I met Jim Lusted for the first time ; the Fiends sound engineer and what an awesome sound he created. Had this wild way out blonde hair do, strongly reminiscent of Bryan Gregory and The Cramps. Jim was a cool guy to have around when ideas were scarce, and he always managed to magic things up exactly when they were needed. The first weekend flew by and in no time at all , I was back in the van heading up the M6 and home to Lytham, but not for long. Nik belled me with the news that my services were required back in the studio putting down new stuff. You Are Soul , Death and Boots On.

Boots On became the most significant song of the session because the flat where the Fiends lived kept getting broken into : it seemed that the burglars actually spent more time there than they did. Nik was well pissed off at this so in an attempt to catch the little shits at it , came up with the hilarious idea of kipping in bed with his boots on. I stayed there one time just after his video and a load of interesting tapes were nicked and was he pissed off ?. " Thieving little bastards !. I've always hated tea leaves ".

Different studio this time around. Terminal twenty four down in The Elephant and Castle, boasting a twenty four track system and two extremely sussed out sound engineers. A guy called Harvey " Porthole " Birrell who shared the workload with our man Jim, in putting down a mindbending session. Kicked off with You Are Soul : same rhythm track as Dead And Buried but in a different key and well messed up. Lot's of hard work , late nights and plenty of Class B that kept us all bright eyed and bushy tailed throughout the session.

Cops turned up at the studio one morning, sending us all into waves of freaking out panic as there was much shit lying around the place. We were down for getting busted for sure, but fortunately, their surprise visit had nothing to do with us : somebody had been stabbed outside the studio and they were sussing out the facts of the incident. Even so they looked on us as well suspicious, with our mindbending thumping music blasting out from the speakers, but the studio manager sorted it and the cops went on their merry little way.

The session ended in giggles and handshakes before shooting back to Brixton and then home for me to chill for a few day's as well as grabbing the chance to take in the vibes of my new situation. Seeing friends and family and solitary walks along Lytham seafront to reflect. My all time

favourite band and there I was jamming in the studios with them. A total contrast to the local live music scene I'd been a part of but even with the new pressures facing me, I knew deep down, all I ever wanted was play drums in a good band and there I was doing it. Now and again, during those lonely walks, I used to get these weird, vivid dreams about playing with the Fiends live, and as fate would have it, premonitions of things to come.

More often than not, they would go like this. The Fiends turn up doing a gig in Blackpool and there I am standing in the crowd waiting for them to appear. The atmosphere slowly building to fever pitch as the gig draws near : suddenly panic and confusion everywhere as the lights go on and the news spreads that their drummer , Johnnie HaHa has slipped down some stairs and broken his arm. My friends in the crowd know how much I'm into the Fiends and push me to the front of the stage telling me to go for it.

I run over to the backstage area where a crowds gathered

The young Andy Wilson !

Maureen and Walt - Mum and Dad !

around Johnnie. I claw my way through in the hope of having a word with Nik ; managing to convince him that I'm the main man for the job. Then all of a sudden there I am. On stage behind Johnnie's drumkit ready for the off. I never once mentioned this dream to Nik in all the time I knew him but it was all pretty weird. Talk about deja vu.

I believe that somebody up there is watching out for each and every one of us at certain times in our lives. I've always maintained that if you stay true to yourself and your ambitions, then good will come your way. Somebody up there was definitely looking down on me with a nice wide smile back then because the call from Nik came through with the skullsnapping news that he'd set up a schedule of tour dates around the UK and Europe and your's truly included in the package.

The news blew my mind. I mean the studio experience was one thing but going on tour with the Fiends playing live. That was a whole new dimension for me to take in but I must have made the right impression on old Nik but I knew what I wanted : knew I was a good drummer in my own right and looked the part from my head to claws. Something Nik recognised in me from the off, and duly grabbed me before somebody else did. It was my twentieth birthday and we partied like mad. Nicci and I met up with friends for a slap up meal ; all concerned ending up very drunk indeed but such a memorable night with the people I loved and cared for.

Nik and Chris had finally had enough of the Brixton experience. The hassle and unwarranted attention had got too much for their little heads to take so they shipped out : Ross Bowmans mother owned a house down in Brighton, so they moved down, which in turn meant Brighton was to be my next port of call : after saying all my goodbyes to friends and family ; plenty of hugs and kisses, I departed with a headful of best wishes from all concerned.

Brighton just happens to be one of those places : liberal thinking, stylish, with oceans of history attached to it. The house was situated on a hilly street and very old. The ideal place for The Fiends to tuck their heads down and chill out after all the hassle of Brixton, but there was another session to get through, so we shot back to London to cram in last minute rehearsals and blow the cobwebs away before heading off to press announcements that Alien Sex Fiend were about to go on tour. It was the greatest buzz of my life knowing I was part of the show I once

and music that kept you rooted to the spot. Colin Irwin of Melody Maker reviewed the bands first sessions ; summing up perfectly what they were trying to get across when he penned " That's nothing compared with the manic nightmare that is Alien Sex Fiend. They make the Fall sound like ABC , the Birthday Party like The Go Go's , Killing Joke like The Bay City Rollers. I doubt if I have ever heard anything uglier in the name of music. A cult following seems assured ". Hard words, considering the aforementioned bands h a d p o w e r f u l reputations themselves when it came down to doing the business.

Schools Out !

dreamed of being in. Better than anything that feeling. Well almost !.

To me Alien Sex Fiend were truly unique. When live, the nearest thing to an out of body experience going as anyone who witnessed our mindbending shows will testify : manic psychotically deranged skullsnapping terror gore theatre at it's peak, mixed in with a Hammer Horror set featuring luminous lighting that enveloped the stage with an eerie glow. With added dimensions of powerful pulsing, grinding electro industrial music that snapped your bones, and Nik's cheeky cockney " awright mate " attitude , it was the perfect cocktail of horror , humour

And he was dead right when he penned those words. The Fiends attracted one of the most fiercely loyal alternative cult following any band could wish for whenever they took the stage. Some nights they even scared the shit out of me, whenever we tripped the light fantastic on stage for another mindblowing show : they always sharpened up their fangs for the evening ; baying for blood at the mere sight of us. But how did it all come about ? This ugliness that Colin Irwin wrote about wayback in 1982 ?.

It has to be looked on as another of those classic rock n roll accidents where like minded souls just happen to meet up and take it from there. The right place at the right time. The Fiendish couple had moved into a North London flat and soon, they were being annoyed by these loud, kinda weird electro sounds growling out from under the floorboards. After investigations, lo and behold, they come across their future guitarist Yaxi. He in turn has a good mate who was a bit handy on the drum machine and the rest is. . . . . . well I don't need to spell it out for you !

The early Alien Sex Fiend line up was formed and they soon acquired a reputation as a band who knew the score ; completing some memorable gigs in the beginning of December 1982 at London's temple of Goth culture The Batcave with their cohorts in musical crime Specimen. The Fiends were out there breaking all the barriers of conventionality : firing up a musical chainsaw and slicing through the industry with a cold hearted psychotic vengeance. Right out there on the edge of insanity ; freaking all the heads out with their disturbing blend of pulsing music and horror theatre with old Nik himself leading them straight to hell. The perfect frontman for the job at hand. There couldn't have been anybody else ; he was tailor made for it Old Nik.

Out popped the Fiends first cassette titled The Lewd The Mad The Ugly and Old Nik. They signed to Cherry Red records and their first release followed shortly : a twelve inch single called Ignore The Machine, with a b-side The Girl At The End Of My Gun. Who's Been Sleeping In My Brain was the first LP and from

these

A case of early tunnel vision ?!

two early releases, the Fiends embarked on their first tour with Specimen getting good reviews along the way. Nik had cracked open his shell and was stretching his wings.

Right from the off I was tuned into their vibes. Nobody I listened too sounded remotely near where this lot were at. Nik the singer with his gaunt ghoulish white facial features and darkened deranged eyes : a mixture of Christopher Lee and a great white shark plus the humour of Herman Munster mixed with the insanity of Alice Cooper, his all time rock idol by the way. And underneath, this continual subliminal effervescence of cockney awright mate humour that made him so brilliant. Especially during showtime when he stepped up ten gears and took everything in a perfect stride.

Nik was all these crazy, complex characters mixed together under one skin a man of ever changing emotional extremities. When he was good he was without doubt the best : when he was bad, he could get very very angry indeed, both to outsiders and people close to him. We, the band members who helped him stir the ingredients of his never ending mental recipe he was cooking, often felt the razor sharp end of his manic fits of raging temper sparked off by the tiniest mishap. Short violent bursts of pure insanity when he flipped out, and when he did flip, he flipped bigtime.

I hope that Nik himself would be the first to admit that as a singer in the true sense of the word, he couldn't sing to save his life but what he did have was a voice that left a presence inside you : one you never forgot that carried him along in the same way as Lydon's did. Shrieking, manic and instantly Nik Fiend. His banshee screams and werewolf growls seemed to carry things along so gracefully at times that it would overwhelm me. A voice containing an all consuming powerful energy that blew away all who stood before as it boomed out from the speakers and embedded itself in your brain.

And the sultry Mrs Fiend backing him up on keyboards : way way beyond the norm to have a woman in the band back in the eighties but Chris added a much needed injection of elegant sexy female gothic to the band. The sounds she dragged out of her keyboards were awesome and this dimension more than compensated for the lack of a bass. Another bold step to take and similar to the concept the Cramps used to good effect. There was so much stuff going on when the Fiends were going for it that a bass just wasn't needed but now and again, Chris did do bass keyboard stuff when it

was called for.

CRASH BANG BANG!!. The most powerful sound imaginable emanated from her keyboards : a mix between a Roland SH 101 and a Juno. thumping pulses that battered you into a coma if you were stood anywhere near the speakers. Only Duran Duran and Depeche Mode were doing similar stuff at the time but they were chart stuff. Safe and acceptable with no danger attached to them : take them home to meet Mummy for afternoon tea and cucumber sandwiches, whereas Nik. Well you wouldn't dare take him home to meet Mum cause he'd bite her head off. . well maybe!

And Yaxi with his unique guitar sounds, a galaxy away from the conventional sounds the instrument could make ; the sound he created would burn through the stage, melt the speakers and ooze into your brain. Mega distortion suffused with tons of reverb : the distinctive twang of early Bryan Gregory boneyard riffs that shivered your timbers. And Johnnie HaHa : now this was more my department as we were both drummers and shared a common interest. He was such an innovator when it came down to drum machines ; his ruthless beats were so solid and yet adventurous at the same time. Lot's of Garry Glitter tribal voodoo beats thrown in for good measure. Primeval and cannibalistic if you catch my drift. Something I always loved about him plus the fact he had the coolest haircut in the band.

For me an instant love affair as soon as I heard that first cassette. A band I was totally into that had all the energy, the youthful exuberance to pull off playing messed up dressed up music. The music press labelled us gothic rock, but the Fiends never really were classic goth rock in comparison to the other black white, doom and gloom bands of the time. We were far too colourful both musically and visually to be classed as such, but the media have to label things : store them away in nice convenient pigeonholes for future reference so we became a goth rock band and that was that. End of story.

Nik was a great interractor with his devoted fans ; giving out just enough of himself to demand undying loyalty and devotion in return from them. From being a fan club member, I was in awe of the guy and all his cosmic ideas and the first time I actually met Nik in person was such a buzz for me. The local band I ended up joining ; the Turnpike Cruisers were booked in for support to the Fiends so I tagged along for the ride in the hope of meeting the man. Even had a brief chinwag with him while we watched Alice Cooper going through eighteen on the big screen. All done up and wearing thigh high

In Between Dreams

leopardskin boots.

Tuss Murray , an old mate of mine was doing a spot of roadying for the Cruisers so I went along to help out. Worked out pretty well as we both wanted to see the Fiends badly. Johnnie HaHa was going through his usual pretentious thing before taking to the stage : over protective with his drumkit but eventually conceding defeat by letting the Cruisers drummer Johnny Moran use them. I was sat on the stairs next to a seven foot coffin listening to the Fiends soundchecking and awesome they were too. The gig was spinetingling despite some scouser flinging red dye all over the place. Nevertheless, a brilliant intro to my future life with the Fiends.

Fanclub news dropped through the door one day informing us the Fiends were about to set off on a UK tour and booked in for an appearance at Clouds nightspot in Preston. The Maximum Security Tour but this time minus the services of their drummer Johnnie HaHa who'd quit the band to concentrate on his hairdressing career. He was such a hard act to follow, that I seriously wondered how they were going to cope without him but no sweat. The Fiends turned adversity around ; going down the same musical avenue, but more hypnotically soothing with it yet still hitting you right between the balls.

I belled the record company and asked them if I could get to meet him properly after the Preston gig and they okayed it. Before the gig I found myself backstage with Suzy the Fiends road manager who was brilliant to me. She took me upstairs, as Yaxi was coming down. He totally blanked me though but he was always a bit of a moody bastard and hated northerners. I liked his perverted sense of humour though, reminding me of my own in so many ways. What a great meeting : getting stoned with Nik and Chris and talking about Alice, the Cramps, horror movies and all kinds of shit. The gig was excellent even without Johnnie and loads of rockabillies turned up. The place erupted and instead of the support band these strippers came on stage for no apparent reason. Very strange !

Meanwhile, back on the local music scene one night during a Turnpikes rehearsal , John Bentham , the manager turned up to see how things were ticking along. I used to be bored rigid going through the same old stuff so in between, I'd throw in a few Fiend beats to keep me amused. John pulled me to one side and said he had some really good news for me. The Turnpikes had support slot for The Fiends and the first gig was scheduled at The Klub Foot in Hammersmith. That was in 1986 and on the Halloween night too. Spooky stuff.

The perfect opportunity for me to get closer to Nik and the Fiends. There were about fifteen hundred people at the Hammersmith gig including three women who turned up at the venue in a hearse ; nice touch ! The Turnpikes gig was excellent and after the show, I had a brief chat with Nik backstage who was well surprised to see me : more importantly to discover I was drumming with the Turnpikes. The next meeting was to be up in Bonnie Scotland where John

Bentham and his crew were filming the Fiends gig live. A great venue with a chunky PA and sounding blistering.

Pre - gig preparations were well hectic and as Yaxi finished doing his bit , Ross Bowman shouted over to me to get my kit up on stage, which looked the business : everywhere burnt out televisions , mannequins and dustbins sprayed up in a multitude of different colours and of course, the legendary muslin cobwebs hanging all over the place.

I started soundchecking and suddenly realised the difference going through top class gear. My drums never sounded so good and I went for it with that feeling inside me once again ; telling me to go for it and fuck everything else. So I banged into RIP with a vengeance and then messed around with a few more Fiendish tunes. Dead And Buried. New Christian Music and other voodoo beats. I was in my element and then some. The gig with The Turnpikes turned out to be quite a strange affair with a very hostile audience giving it loads. " Get the fuck off the stage and get the Fiends on " and that kind of thing. The Fiends appeared to William Tells overture and the jocks went berserk, freaking out everywhere : they loved the Fiends with a passion and there was always a strong anarchistic vibe to them whenever we went north of the border. They all waited and wanted a taste of the new single too ; Hurricane Fighter Plane but it was a " not tonight Josephine " for the jocks.

Backstage after the gig we all got severely wasted but

somehow, through the alcoholic cloud, I managed to get into Nik's ribs, spending quite a bit of time yakking away and telling him how weird it felt drumming in the support band to the Fiends. Nik told me they were going off to check out Alice Coopers " The Nightmare Returns " gigs and that Alice hadn't ruled the UK since 1982 so we all said our goodbyes to one another before shooting off to Lytham for a well earned rest.

Then some truly amazing fuck off news happened for the Fiends. After a backstage meeting with Alice they received a call from his record company offering them the final seven shows supporting " coops". Zodiac Mindwarp went blind at the last minute : Doctor And The Medics pulled out and there was much confusion but the Fiends jumped in and played a strict thirty five minute set but sadly, I missed all the shows due to commitments in Holland with the Cruisers. Didn't stop me being pleased for Nik though : always a massive fan of the " coops " and his fantasy was to turn into him one day.

Nik made the daily papers with headlines like. . . . Alice is saved by his Fiends. Is there a strange curse striking down the bands that support shock rocker Alice Cooper ?. It was too good a chance for Nik to miss out on to realise his childhood dream : when he was thirteen he saw Alice play in his hometown and dreamed that one day he would appear on the same stage as the man himself.

I arrived back from Holland to spend some time at home chilling out with Nicci : the girl who I fell in love with ; who later became my wife. She was in a flat in Lytham above a record store : the owner of which always made sure I received the latest sounds ; spending many a pleasant hour together drinking tea , getting stoned and listening to music. Christmas comes but once a year and it was that time of year. After spending some of the festivities down in London ; indulging in excesses of nostril business and alcohol I headed back to Lytham for peace and quiet. Prior to my leaving London I telephoned my Mum to wish her all the best and she told me Nik had phoned wanting to speak to me.

Maybe the feelings I was getting were signs of things to come. I wasn't sure but I remember John Bentham mentioning that there could be a possibility of the Cruisers supporting the Fiends for the rest of their UK tour. But then again why had Nik phoned me personally :

Nicci and Rat - caught in a dream

surely he would go through John the manager to sort out Turnpike business wouldn't he ?. Talk about jumping around. Then the telephone rang : I flew downstairs and grabbed it. It was Nik on the line asking me what I was doing New Year with the Cruisers and making me green with envy with Alice Cooper ditties. I told him things were a bit quiet but there was the possibility of some gigs coming up. Nothing concrete though.

And then right in the bollocks !!. I couldn't fuckin' believe it. He's asking me if I'd like to come down to London and have a jam with the Fiends. Nothing too heavy. Just some drumming , drinking and smoking. I told him I'd love the chance and after calming down , he told me he'd be sending a guy called Ross Bowman, to collect my drumkit and anything else I needed and then, bring me back to London for a session.

I called Nicci pronto to tell her the good news : she was so happy for me because she knew from the off, I wanted in with the Fiends so badly and now here was my big chance to prove to myself and them that I could do the business well enough. Being in love with Nicci and the spellbinding news from Nik made me feel on top of the world. One of the times when I felt it was all worth it. All the years my Mum ; god bless her, had suffered me blasting out earbending punk music, in between screaming at me to get a job : my brother Steve who'd taken over as Dad used to give me plenty of shit for being myself. I just felt vindicated, now I was going down to rehearse with the Fiends and prove to myself and

family it had all been worth it.

The following day I called to see Richard King, the frontman with the Cruisers to tell him the news that I'd be withdrawing my services forthwith. He was well pleased for me and after shaking hands , I called round to see John Bentham to give him the good news. He sat there giving me all this wise understanding Fatherly advice but underneath it all , John as did many more of my mates, seemed to know exactly what was going on. As it turned out , Nik had belled John and asked about me and John to his credit told Nik that I could do the business on the drums. He didn't have to do that for me, and I will always have the highest respect for John for wording Nik up in such a way.

Nicci and Rat - zombified !

So it was a few days later that Ross Bowman turned up outside my door after a treacherous drive from London. Snow had hit the country really bad and I thought he wasn't going to make it because of the heavy fall, but Ross was one of those guys : if a job needed doing then he would do it. A very sound guy indeed Mr Bowman, and I couldn't have asked for a better guy to begin my dream with as we picked our way through the freezing cold night down to London.

CHAPTER TWO

Smells Like...

With the exit of Johnnie, the original Alien Sex Fiend drummer, we faced the task of altering our style. Forced to use the drum machine as a filler for the rhythm : I entered the frame having to cope with playing over two tracks, which was very challenging for me to get my head round. Yaxi loved playing the arsehole : had this nasty habit of controlling the main drum tracks and kicking them out of synch whenever he needed confusion but that was Yaxi. Mister fuckin' wind up.

With a tight new sound, we were more than ready to fuck with the world : claws sharpened and hungry for prey. Okay, the record deal was in place but behind the scenes, we faced the endless aggro of organising vans , promo material and tons more. All this came as a shock but I soon became accustomed to Nik's way of working, which at times was very fuckin' chaotic but that's the way he was. Mountains out of molehills instead of taking things cool and sorting out the shit as it hit the fan. Everyone jumped in to help out whenever work needed to be done, in between endless spliffs and cups of tea.

New faces were popping up the whole time to make their presence known to me. Paul "Benny" Bainbridge, the lighting engineer ; a naturally funny guy who spliffed like it was out of fashion. He used to set up the stage lighting as if at any moment , the Predator was about to burst out and bite your head off. On the Maximum Security Tour we still had the prison cell and his party piece was to stick his head through the window and freak everybody out while on stage. Other faces in the Fiends roadcrew were Moz and Skins from Leeds. Moz was Mrs Fiends keyboard magician and stagehand who made sure she was always sorted. At nearly seven foot tall a real friendly giant but very handy to have around whenever trouble lurked. Skins was always a laugh on tour doing our heads in with his pig impersonations. A trick he picked up from the farm he worked on, between touring. Josh sorted Yaxi out ; making sure his guitar always sounded boneyard dirty. A right pair of silly fuckers when they were on one ; taking the piss out of anyone who stood in their way.

Andy from Sheffield , who sold tee shirts, before promotion to the lofty rank of drum and guitar doctor. A great guy who usually kept himself to himself : he loved being pissed out of his head and getting his meat and two veg away whenever the chance appeared. To back up the brilliant Jim Lusted on sound was the equally brilliant Billy Young who'd been there with the Fiends since the year dot. The tour accountant and sorter outer, whenever there was stuff to sort : your typical safeguard on tour and a guy we called on countless times to pull us out of the shit. Billy always reminded me of Sid James the way he went about his business. A very funny man to have around in any situation.

So there we were, all ready to kick arse. On the tour we were accompanied by a very special guest ; Baron Puppet from the Big Apple. A cool hip hop rapper Nik and Chris met in a club and asked him if he'd like to jump on board

Ratti and Baron Puppett-robbed again !

the tour. Our new single Hurricane Fighter Plane had just been released and we were all raring to go. The first gig was Leamington Spa and very civilised it was too. I got to the stage to soundcheck and Benny and Skins sorted out my drumkit. I had two six hundred watt speakers either side of me : I always liked my music loud but this was fuckin' outrageous.

The roadcrew got stuck into a load of food and we all shot off to a restaurant with the promoter. Kids were hanging around outside asking for autographs ; that kinda thing. When we arrived back at the venue we were rushed down a side alley to the backstage area, due to the street being crammed full of goths , punks , and hair do's all trying to catch a glimpse of the band. Half an hour before showtime, so out came the crimpers and make up : spliffed up and sank a few long glasses of Jack to get me into the mood of playing my first live gig with Alien Sex Fiend.

The crowd were banging on the stage and throwing obscenities at everybody as they waited for us to take the stage. Billy would always come into the dressing room and in a very official voice announce to us all " ten minutes ". He did this

everytime and it freaked me out how he could be so cool about it all. Five minutes to go and there I was swallowing enough Jack to sink a battleship. We were nearly ready : Mrs Fiend looking elegant in crushed purple velvet dress and Nik with his white panstick gaunt looking face and spiky beehive hair do. And Yaxi looking like the bailiffs had just called round and confiscated all his worldly belongings : looking mean , nasty and desperate as if he was ready to fuck with the world. And there was me. Freaked out and feeling like the voodoo doctor had cast one of his wicked spells on me.

Seconds later I was living the dream. The lights dimmed : the dry ice suffocated the stage area as The Fiends took to the stage to rapturous applause , psychotic screams and banshee-like wails of approval from the mental crowd gathered below. I couldn't see shit so Moz helped me over to my drumkit and all I remember was feeling sick and nervous. Total panic as we kicked into the first song of the set. . . . April Showers from the IT album.

I calmed myself ; starting off the slow stomping clockwork beat as the audience swayed from side to side waiting for old Nik. Then from a corner of the stage , bathed in an eerie ghostly glow he appeared and the noise doubled in intensity. The Messiah had come again to stalk the stage with his irrepressible presence. Nicking as many fags as he could get between his fingers in the process from the sweat soaked crowd. The whole place exploded as we tore into them with a skullsnapping bend over

Beethoven beat. Bottles , items of clothing and just about everything flew our way as we stormed into "wop bop ". People were on the stage as the security men booted them off. Even Nik laid into a few of them with his plates of meat and getting right off on it at the same time. We ended the song and the crowd didn't give themselves time to recover as up next was the classic RIP. We didn't give them time to breathe.

" Nurse!. Get me a fuckin' bedpan. Stop banging nails in my lid " : Nik was throwing himself all over the gaff and running into my drumkit like some demented lemming on acid. Cymbals and mikestands crashed onto the floor and on stormed the roadies to sort it while I sat behind the remains, checking out the mayhem. This was showtime Alien Sex Fiend style with the crowd loving every second of it. It was complete fuckin' chaos in Leamington Spa, like the lunatics had finally managed to take over the asylum and there was I smack bang in the middle of it loving every second of it.

This is what I'd always dreamed of and it was better than I ever imagined it would be. The two together : the agony and the ecstasy mixed together to make one insane cocktail. Nik was screaming like some crazed banshee. " I know nothing. Nothing no more. RIP. RIP. RIP ". Towards the end of the song I started feeling really weird and before I knew it , I woke up with my head next to a strobelight and the monitor ; totally fucked out of my head.

Next thing I know. Ross was helping me up, asking if I was okay or not. I told him to get me a glass of Jack with loads of ice . I think I just got a touch over excited and passed out. Plus, it was so fuckin' hot in there that night ; the heat given off from the lights surrounding the drumkit was unbelievable ; like being stuck in the Sahara desert or drumming on a sun bed.

There were over fifteen hundred people at that gig and I think all the Fiend fans really got off on the fact there were live drums back in the band. The sound must have totally fried their bacon doing stuff like Wild Women and Boneshaker Baby. Afterwards, we enjoyed an intimate party back in the dressing room with a few fans coming through to join us. It was weird signing autographs and all that but something that was worthwhile for both the band and the fans. We stayed in the hotel that night and got thoroughly wasted before moving on.

Leeds next, and a gig I can't remember much about but I do recall it was at The Ritzy in this shopping complex affair : once again a mental crowd turned up to see us doing the business. A load of

Rat in action

skinheads turned up too, wanting a rumble so we fired into Dead and

Rat drumming up support at the Klub Foot , Hammersmith

Buried and they got one. Moz and Skins were from Leeds so understandably a lot of their mates appeared to sample the unique flavour of a Fiend recipe. Had a riot too but I didn't meet any of Skins pigs though !

The tour bus was always full of good humour, music and spliffs to chill us out from all the mayhem of the shows , along with the usual barrage of piss taking courtesy of Yaxi and Josh. Baron Puppet was a naturally funny guy and we got on well together : always ready to hear his colourful stories of Big Apple life. We indulged in a fair bit of gambling the Baron and I, but I soon learned my lesson after ending up skint after many a session.

Shellys in Stoke was the next venue : can't really recall anything too spectacular about this little gathering. While on tour I never failed to keep in contact with the people back home. Keeping Nicci constantly wired as to how things were progressing with the Fiends. I told her the news we were playing Manchester soon and that she should try to get over to see the show ; putting her on the guest list just in case.

Next stop Milton Keynes. . . .now

this place was fuckin' weird : as we arrived we came across the world famous concrete cows out in the fields chewing the cud. No mad cows disease for that herd ever. It was very very bizarre. Paul Weller summed it up perfectly when he wrote Strange Town. That futuristic excuse for a town could well have been the inspiration behind the pen.

The venue was bang in the town centre. Called The Point ; it was a pyramid shaped building with a good stage area and when we kicked off the gig the whole building was suddenly full of smoke. Naturally !. The Fiends were at it again but not our fault. The club owners failed to open up the roof vents so as a result, clouds of dense smoke lay everywhere. The cops turned up pretty sharpish thinking the building was on fire: must have looked mental from the outside. This trippy pyramid looking like it was all set for blast off to the moon.

Did a storming version of Hurricane Fighter Plane and Smells Like Shit that evening. Baron Puppet went down well with the audience really getting off on him. He came off the stage feeling very pleased with himself as we all did. A great gig in a very weird town but it was Manchester next. Home of the Red Gods and Boddingtons bitter. Family and friends were turning out for this one including my delectable Nicci and we were scheduled to play at the International. A venue that was to say the least, a bit of a shithole but a reputation second to none.

And what a hot sweaty affair that night turned out to be. Packed to the rafters and all set for a serious head pumping session we ripped into a barrage of brain damaging tunes : I could see a few of my mates piled on top of each other going fuckin' mental and giving me loads of shit in the process. " Rats a wanker " and other cheeky banter but they were having a good time. All part and parcel of it so I just came back with a "yeah right. I'm up here and you ain't so fuck right off ". All done in the best possible taste and no harm meant.

Some way into the set : Shock horror ! I could see Moz lifting Nicci off the floor so I wondered what the fuck was happening to her. She'd passed out onto the monitor desk after things got a little too much for her. After the gig we all indulged in a right old knees up with my mates who'd come to see if I really was drumming with the Fiends and not just spinning a few porkies here and there.

After a night in a hotel and breakfast , Bristol was about to fall under siege from the Fiends. Our spirits were high after a memorable Manchester gig. This part of the tour saw us completing seven shows as Nik decided to split it up in two parts. Bristol was a lot of fun but that was about it really apart from some people dangling from the roof dancing in cages but as to why they were , I still don't know. Very strange goings on.

Liverpool next and scheduled to play in The Grafton Rooms in a well dodgy part of a town. The venue was like a nineteen sixties dance hall if you will; for some reason vivid flashbacks of them all bopping away to Bill Haley came into my mind because that era was all around that venue. The weird stagnant smells of faded social history gave it an eerie atmosphere and I wanted out badly, but there was business to do so it was case of stay don't run.

Tons of problems with the PA system and the people who owned the venue. This guy called Tony was a total wanker just because we didn't fit in with his ideas of what a band should look and sound like. Not his usual run of the mill rock bands he was used to dealing with and he , along with his crew of dickhead mates made it their business to go out of their way to be thoroughly fuckin' nasty to us. As the night wore on Nik was beginning to get a tad pissed off with his attitude as a lot of heads had turned up to see the gig and Nik wanted to be on top form. They were all in the audience : punks , skins , goths , you name it : the whole alternative youth culture of Liverpool had turned out en masse to see us that night.

More PA problems made the crowd angry. They'd come to see a show and it was all down to that wanker Tony playing head games with us. The gig ended and we survived , thanks to security and one of the guys , an ex-boxer pleaded with us to take him on board the starship Sex Fiend but sadly, no chance. We left Liverpool with a bad taste ; trying hard to tried to fuck Tony off with threats of hiring a replacement PA company but there was only one gig remaining so what the fuck.

Keele up next, and for me, a flavourless gig. Sure, a lot of kids had turned up to see us and a good time was had by all but there was something missing. Maybe because it was the last show of the tour I don't know but I didn't feel my normal RatFink self. If any of you have a copy of The Germs LP with the picture of Nik and I together pointing at the camera and Nik doing his best Rat impression , that is where the piccie comes from. My drumkit ended up scattered all over the stage ; completely dismembered and what a pleasant way to end a gig !

Afterwards, we headed straight down to Brighton. No lounging around in hotels ; just pack up the gear in the van and do one out of there. We all crashed down in the back of the van until we hit Brighton leaving Nik and Chris to chill out in bed together on our arrival. Paul and I had a look round some shops and cafes and strolled along the Brighton seafront for ages with a smoke to chill the pair of us right out.

The Fiends only had a couple of days in which to relax before hopping on the ferry and heading off on my first European tour with them and one that kicked off in Paris at The Rex Club. The ferry crossing was mental and we all got completely bladdered and yours truly ended the journey puking my guts up as a result of my excesses. It took about four hours to hit Paris so I used the time wisely ; managing to get my head down en route and recover from my cross Channel binge. Woke up feeling well refreshed listening to the weird strains of Captain Beefhearts Clearspot.

Our arrival in Paris was greeted by a well enthusiastic promoter who took us to this trippy restaurant after checking in at the hotel. " Ooohh La La " : French cuisine and Nik insisted we all get a few frogs legs down our necks. A plate covered in frogs legs under a creamy white wine and garlic sauce was stuck under my nose and after the initial horror had passed , they did taste amazingly good. " Poor little bastards " I thought but yummie little bastards at the same time.

The promoter was raving about us : how the gig had been sold out for ages and that he was so excited the Fiends were on French soil and all the rest of it. I was in Paris so what more could I ask for ?. Nik and Chris played the responsible couple routine and slipped off to the hotel so me and the rest of the crew decided to head off in search of fun and adventure. Found this really dodgy strip joint off the main boulevard and after a unanimous vote , decided to give it a try.

Just your typical Fiend gig !

We scored a bottle of poppers and shared it out between the lot of us , laughing our cocks off at all these strange looking dancers. Yaxi and Josh were getting out of it and up to their usual piss taking business ; shouting at the dancers to come over and sit on their faces, etc etc. A pleasant enough thought but bad news in a strange city. Suddenly these two guys come over and one of them chirps up in a dodgy sounding French accent " If you don't like what you see , then why don't you get the fuck out ". Trouble was brewing but once again, our man Billy sorted in his usual cool collected way ; calming Yaxi and Josh down before we swallowed our beer and a sharp exit.

Waking up with a killer hangover , I discovered the crew had already set off for the gig to do all the gear humping and set the stage up to a Fiendishly correct manner. Nik and Chris were down to be to be interviewed on French radio so they shot off leaving us to hang around until the off. The venue was a pretty weird shape for a club ; narrow and long with the bar at one end. There were people outside already having queued since the afternoon to make sure they got in. Some wait considering the doors weren't scheduled to open until eight. Nik decided on a set change that night and have a go at Girl On The End Of My Gun.

EST Trip To The Moon was a monster favourite with the French Fiends and Nik had warned me the crowds go completely fuckin' mental so I was expecting the worst when we hit the stage but surprised to see them all standing there perfectly still. Weird or what ?. But then as soon as Yaxi kicked in with I Walk The Line , that was it : the whole place went fuckin' ballistic ; running back and forth and grouping up in a big circle and running round each other. It was like a pit of terror and God help anybody who happened to slip into it.

And then disaster struck !!. I looked to my right of the stage, where a large very heavy speaker was falling into the crowd. This was completely insane and I remember people being crushed by huge bass bins : horrendous stuff going on all around me. The promoter and stagehands were running around like headless chickens trying to sort the mess out and as a consequence , the show stopped as people were pulled out and taken off to hospital.

Nik thought " fuck this one" ; shouting to the remaining members of the audience that there was a girl on the end of his gun. We went into chaos orbit once again. " Do ya wanna die ?. Kill kill kill !! ". The whole place erupted and the adrenalin surge was fuckin' awesome. Like the best drug going : Nik knew exactly how to crank up the crowd and from potential disaster he turned the situation round and got them all right back up there. He really pulled it together that night in Paris and one of the memories I have of Nik that will never leave me. A true showman in every sense of the word.

We later discovered one guy had broken his arm and three others had suffered concussion : the promoter was freaking out and heaping all the blame on us but we were having none of it. " Fuck him" we thought. if he can't sort out the club in a safe manner then that's his problem. He should have realised it would be chaotic with the show being sold out well before the off. I mean we were the Fiends playing to our loyal army of fans ; what did he expect ?. Barry Manilow ?. Dammed good show though even though it could have been better organised.The Eiffel Tower was awesome and we all spliffed out while looking down on the magnificent city of Paris, five hundred feet up in the air and a fitting finale to our Parisian business. Au Revoir Paris !!. Next up Belgium ; the home of Stella lager and chocolates. The tour was zipping along swimmingly with most of the shows sold out and the chance to meet loads of different Euro heads and sleeping in comfortable beds too. What happened in Belgium did my fucking lid in. Without a doubt the scariest moments of my life were lived out on the streets of Belgium. We'd just done the business in Antwerp and our spirits were up and ready for anything : took in a nice long spliffing session as we made our way to Brussels. A great hotel was waiting for us with a way out reception area , marble floors and gold trimmings everywhere. Almost felt like royalty as we checked in.

Outside the Eiffel Tower in Paris

After a quick wash and brush up, we met up with the promoter downstairs in the foyer to talk business. She had booked us a couple of tables at this cool restaurant in the centre of town. Very extravagant with loads of colourful salads and meat dishes swilled down with very tricky cocktails. One of them was appropriately called a zombie and turned out to be my favourite. Came in a large glass bowl full of Tequila and fruity things and we all ended up getting severely pissed.

The promoter suggested we go to this bar where she and her business cohorts hung out whenever they were downtown looking for action. The bar was situated in a small alley off the main drag full of shops , strip clubs and gay bars. Very sexy area of the world where an imaginative soul could indulge in all kinds of personal fantasies. We got ourselves a cosy corner of the bar and discussed the details while soaking up the vibes of being in a strange town. How things were going; was the promoter pleased with ticket sales and all the other stuff and were told the good news that all the shows had been sold out so it was wide smiles and drinks all round.

Now this bar had one of those vibes to it : laced with a dodgy tense uptight vibe like it could go off at any second. There was a mob of beefy looking blokes clocking us from the other side of the bar but by that time I was wasted so couldn't really suss what the fuck was going on and wouldn't have been able to jump in if anything did kick off. Couldn't even make eyeball contact I was that gone.

Yaxi and Josh get up and decide to try their hand out on the pinball machine before slipping into their usual wind up mode : Yaxi gobbing off in his loud annoying cockney accent thinking he's the dogs bollocks and slowly going OTT to all the people in the bar. After finishing fuckin' around on the machines he staggered back to where we were sat and crashed down looking well worse for wear.

We thought we'd call it a night and scoot back to the hotel to catch some zzzz's so our heads were sorted for the following day. Yaxi sits down smoking a fag and drinking his beer, when suddenly one of the beefs come over to us and decides to sit down in Yaxi's lap giving him loving hugs and kisses at the same time. This guy who was massive and a skinhead to boot , sat on Yaxi, looking like he was going to start fuckin' him any moment. A strange vibe was building up all around and even though we tried to laugh it off , it wasn't having it. Then WALLOP !!. Beefy massive skinhead butts poor old out of order Yaxi smack in the kisser : we all stood up to sort it out and then his mates decide to come over thinking their mate was about to take a kicking from these bizarre looking creatures.

SHIT !!. They were about a dozen strong and all between eighteen to twenty stones in weight. Your worst fuckin' nightmare about to come true but this one was happening and how. Yaxi stood his ground and wasn't having any of it and as we hit the street , decided to go for it ; jumping on this huge bloke like he meant it. Well that was it. Fuckin' pandemonium broke out all around and we all braced ourselves for a proper kicking from the Belgium beefcakes.

One of their mates , an awesome looking Chuck Norris style monster went into warp factor : taking up this martial art combat stance like he'd done it a thousand times before and kicking and punching anybody who got in his way. Skins and Billy took the brunt of this guy right in the face. Josh in the meantime was going through the horrendous reality of being thrown through a plate glass window of a well busy gay bar. Glass all over the show and these blokes from inside the bar where Josh landed freaking out completely. Harvey had managed to leg it down an alley with two beefcakes in hot psychotically deranged pursuit. They catch him and proceed to give him a good old stomping ; dragging him to the floor and laying into him with fists and boots.

It's quite a tough one for me to describe the terrifying feeling as to what was going on all around me that night. It was like something out of Clockwork Orange but worse ; like the world had gone completely fuckin' crazy. Anyway Jim was stood right in front of me getting the seven shades kicked out of him so I decided it was my time to join in and do my bit. No other choice really. In the meantime Nik and Chris were well out of it ; at the other end of the alley with the promoter not realising for a second that his band was being ripped apart. "Fuck this " I thought and launched into this bloke who was punching Jim and started laying into him with a vengeance. This bloke didn't flinch a fuckin' inch as I pummelled away on his head like it was my drumkit.

" Shit. He's gonna turn around and rip my fuckin' head off any second now ". Suddenly I hear Billy screaming at me. . . ." Ratty. For fucks sake. DUCK ". Instinct took over for some reason and I immediately hit the deck as a sheet of glass shattered into a million crystals inches above me. I had spiky hair at the time and I could feel the glass skim ominously through my hair like the hand of death when the reaper calls up your number. That was it. With my best Ben Johnson head on I got up and legged it like I'd never legged it before. Nobody would have caught me that night ; not even Linford Christie on a good one.

I never did go a bundle on legging it whenever the shit hit the fan but that night I had no other option open to me. It was a case of stay and get kicked to fuck or run and play the gig tomorrow. No contest really but even so , running away wasn't really my thing. I suppose it was the Man United in me. The stay don't run mentality the Red Army had when facing an off. All the time I was pounding down the street with these fuckin' skinheads on my tail , like a pack of hungry wolves out for blood. I was wishing the impossible : if only our Steve was here with me now. Even though we'd have only been two handed , we'd have sorted the bastards out no sweat.

Our kid was a legend back home : a Lambretta riding Man United supporting looney . A very tasty geezer when it came down to aggro and looking back , the reason why I was pounding down that street as if my life depended on it. Steve had been responsible not only for family matters but for my musical direction ; my mentor who always gave me encouragement , always turned up with the latest impossible to get sounds after trips to America and the one who pushed me into the local band scene. He wouldn't have had any of it that night in Belgium but he wasn't there and I was so it was a case of he who runs away lives to fight another day. A stupid saying but one that sums up that horrendous night perfectly for me.

Got myself around the corner where Nik and Chris were and lo and behold, the hotel was in sight and safety. I puked up everywhere. My stomach in knots and breathless from all the aggro. Billy had managed to catch up with us outside the hotel and explained to me what had happened. A piece of triangular shaped glass had been plucked from the broken window by one of the skinheads who then came at me using it like a broadsword. If Billy hadn't have been around to warn me , then I wouldn't have been around. The glass would have took my fuckin' head off for sure and that would have been end of story for sure. I owe my life to Billy and still retain

Down to the bare essentials...

the utmost respect for him even though it's been some time since our paths last crossed.

The rest of the lads made it back to base in one piece : admittedly looking a right fuckin' mess but at least they were alive. We all got together in the hotel foyer to catch our breath from the ultra violence : I imagined the skinheads laying siege to us locked in the hotel. Doing an Assault On Precinct Thirteen on us until they'd killed every last fuckin' Sex Fiend they could get their hands on. Skins had a very nasty split above his left eye left eye and the receptionist was scared shitless wondering what had happened to us all. We filled him as to the nights events and he in turn made sure all the doors and windows locked in an attempt to keep out the mental murderous bunch of skinheads.

We got Skins up to one of the rooms and tried to clean up his wound but it needed stitches it was that bad. I remember him lying on a table and blood spurting out all over his face. Proper Hammer Horror stuff. We were well shook after all that; all pale and emotions shook up like somebody had ripped out our insides and stuck them all in one massive liquidiser. Skins was carted off to hospital for attention and ended up with seven stitches for his troubles. The rest of us carried an assortment of cuts , bruises , fat lips and black eyes. I kept thinking about the headlines that thankfully would never be. " Alien Sex Fiend drummer decapitated in Belgium brawl ". Mind you , it would definitely have helped the record sales.

We finally chilled after a couple of spliffs and beers. Nik decided to get the fuck out of Dodge City and quitting the Belgium shows altogether and I for one thought that a brilliant idea. After going through one terrifying ordeal , I did not want to repeat the experience or stay in Belgium one second longer than I had to. In the morning Nik and Chris got on the blower to the promoter and told her the bad news. Then the unbelievable truth came out about the fight : the blokes who'd given us such a vicious kicking were in fact the Fiends very own security guys for the shows. Fuckin' ironic or what ?. To be stomped into Belgian soil by your own blokes. This was indeed outrageous to swallow and every credit to Nik too. He stuck by the decision to quit Belgium even though there was money to be lost. He didn't give a shit. He wanted out

A very goth' Rat

and so we packed up the gear and headed off to a safer and more imaginative place to chill. Amsterdam !

Now this was more like it ; after a long journey we finally arrived in the city of drugs , debauchery , pornography , peep shows , pimps and prostitutes, meandering canals and Van Gogh. Lovely !!. I'd already done the Amsterdam experience with the Turnpikes but this time around , it was a million miles better. It's such a cool laid back place with it's crazy coffee shops and smoking bars. Very civilised and totally spoilt for choice if you are a serious dope smoker in search of brain damaging tackle.

More Fiendish capers...

We were down to play in The Paradiso club and caught the tail end of a tattoo convention just clearing up. Lot's of bikers and skin freaks in from all over the place and showing off their colourful tatts to all and sundry. The gig was to say the least , one of the oddest experiences : all of us well stoned and loads of crazy musical fuck ups along the way. I remember seeing Nik getting handed all kind of things; pipes , bongs , spliffs. You name it and he had it and he comes over to me during the gig and stuck a pipe in my mouth. So funny he was during showtime. A man of emotional extremities : unrehearsed and spontaneous. One gig down and depressed. The next gig up in the cosmos with an in ya face attitude. Not afraid to drop a note and the creator of relentless skullsnapping chaos. The more chaotic it was , the more he thrived. Like Nero playing his fiddle as Rome burned to the ground all around him. I was totally spaced that night as the gig finally came to a close and we crawled out of The Paradiso slaughtered.

We were given the day off so we set off to explore the delights of Amsterdam : Paul , Ross , Myself and Wolfgang the German contact who took care of all the smoking supplies and other essential business items. We finally came across Nik and Chris and went off to the Bulldog cafe which was the biggest coffee shop in in the Dam. Had a crazy chinwag and watched a very weird film. We were down for playing a place called Den Haag the following night : about fifty k's from Amsterdam but I can't remember a thing about that one. Must have been very good !

" EL LOCO !!!! ". The next Fiendish adventure of the European Tour was just around the corner. We needed sunshine to charge up our spiritual batteries after freezing our way through France, the nightmare of Belgium and Holland. Next up was to be one of my favourite places in the world. ESPANIA!!. I'd never been there before but I recall all the times I wanted to visit as a child after watching those holiday programmes and some really cool films set in Spain.

There something totally mystifying to me about Spain. The sun , the colours , the diverse panoramic scenery , the beautiful people and the art : Salvador Dali being one of my favourite artists of all time. So you could say I was very excited about the Spanish trip. We had to endure another long journey but eventually conquered it over three mindbending days of driving with the stench of Yaxi's feet stinking out the tour bus. Still we had some good sounds and spliffs to take our minds off it so it wasn't all bad. As each morning approached , we could feel the warmth getting nearer and the smells of the ocean. Wolfgang jumped in with us too and continually rolled spliffs that would seriously lift your wig off.

The horrors of Belgium paled into insignificance as each mile brought us nearer to Spain and you could feel the vibe between us all getting calmer and much more relaxed. Nik always loved playing Spain and told me stories about how late bands who play there go on stage and how great the people are towards you. Told me all I need to do is to stick the drum machine on and watch the whole fuckin' place erupt. Great stories of the food and the abundance of Charles to anybody who was into nostril business. Yeah , a very civilised place to play.

Arrived at last !. A small town just outside Valencia the name of which escapes me but it was very beautiful with loads of palm trees and whitewashed houses. We checked into the hotel; opened the windows , rolled up a rug and off with the tee shirts. There wasn't a cloud in the sky to be seen and the whole vibe was just perfect. The hotels were so different to others we'd stayed in ; bare with cold marble floors and wooden shutters on the windows and hardly any bedding and bathrooms with powerful jet spas to sooth away your aches and pains and hangovers. Well at least no more smelly feet from Mr Yaxi !!

After a clean up we all met up in the lobby; some things never changed !!. Scooted off downtown to this pleasant coffee bar to meet up with the promoters. The coffee was something else : I'd never tasted beans like them and the strength !. One cup really gave you a kick. No gig that night so it was off to Valencia for the night with the promoter as our host and unofficial tour guide. What a surprise lay ahead for us as we hit Valencia : on each street corner were these huge papier mache sculptures the like of which I'd never seen. Valencia was gripped in the fever of The Phallus Festival (pronounced fayas) and what a scene Dantes Inferno had nothing on Valencia that night.

Amazing ornately detailed sculptures scattered all over the town from wild horses to fat freaky belly dancers and I later discovered there are over a million quids worth of these go into every festival. The whole place goes fuckin' mental for seven days and all around me was the sound of fireworks exploding and crazy parties going off everywhere. We arrived at this bar ; falling out of the cab and to our amazement right outside the bar was this huge cross with a papier mache chicken nailed to it. Now if any of you have the Ignore The Machine single, then that is the picture on the front cover : these crazy Spaniards had gone to the considerable trouble of recreating the front cover outside this crazy bar we found ourselves in.

All these really cool people were coming over to check us out and it felt like we were proper popstars that night. The crew went off to the bar while we sloped off to this crazy intimate bar to meet and chinwag with the promoters and other such people. Out came the champagne by the gallon and then these white bags of Charles to give it more fizz. He had finally arrived and I couldn't wait to sample some. The Spanish love their coke : sitting in a busy restaurant you'd see people with these little silver spoons they use to snort the stuff. All very open and civilised and a total contrast to the attitude over here.

After fifteen minutes I got in a right state trying to talk to all these important people while being off my noodle. I could not stop laughing listening to all these people yakking away in Spanish. Yeah I'd done coke before but this stuff was outrageous : felt like my head was going to lift off my body at any second and after an hour or so of this wig lifting buzz I was experiencing , we finally made a move downtown to another serious wig lifting experience.

Midnight signalled the greatest pyrotechnic show I have ever witnessed : the sky awash with millions of shimmering fragmented colours that was just so spectacular to see. Hundreds of people all running around screaming and dancing and then the final act. The setting fire to all the sculptures , some of which were over twenty five feet high. The whole town felt like it was ablaze as the sculptures burned away and I almost felt sorry for them. All that work going in to create beautiful works of art ; destroyed in minutes by the licking flames. A strangely moving totally unexpected evening I will never forget. Spectacular but weird with it. Just the way I like life to be now and again.

The gig in Valencia turned out to be exactly the fandango Nik told me it would be : the Spanish don't think of partying till around the witching hour and our arrival was greeted by by a tumult of blasting car horns and lot's of crazy dancing in the street. The whole place went fuckin' wild with crazed enthusiasm as we walked in. The venue was mirrored wall to wall and raised platforms everywhere and bathed in ultra violet light and lot's of semi naked bodied flying around as we ripped into Hurricane Fighter Plane with venomous attitude. Quite a

Rat models the Captain Sensible look

straight looking audience compared to our usual bunch of gaunt rotting corpses : a healthy good looking bunch with well tanned bodies and dressed well. We didn't kick off until around four in the morning and before the gig indulged in mucho nostril business , spliffidge and alcohol to chill us.

The Spanish tour consisted of two shows ; one in Valencia and the other in Alicante so not much hassle there organising and transporting the gear around. Bit like a holiday really and what better place to holiday in. The promoters were very cool with us and provided us all with little treats along the way. Lot's of ice cold Spanish beers filled the cooler in the tour bus to keep us all thoroughly refreshed as we headed off to Alicante. Arrival saw us all feeling pretty numb : the sun was a glorious deep orange colour and baking hot. We were directed to this shabby arena called Mana Mana and a good half an hour from the metropolis.

Shot off to the hotel for some much needed Spanish nosh and consumed platefulls of Paella and mucho glasses of Vino. Stuffed ourselves as much as we could before we headed back to Mana Mana and showtime. Outside the club were these huge poles on which were stuck eyeballs of varying sizes and colours; it all looked fuckin' mental. The club was a huge room with a removable roof , two bars on either side and no carpet ; only sand. Kicked off with a neckstrangling version of You Are Soul and the whole place took off. The owners asked us if we'd do two sets so we agreed ; coming off at five to return at six for more

business. Dry ice engulfed the stage and the roof came off leaving me a spectacular view of the stars as I drummed away thinking this is what life is all about. Three thousand people that night and there was no stopping them. Just no stopping them !

After one crazy nostril business party in the dressing room followed by a boogie in the club itself when we bopped till we dropped , we finally managed to stagger out of Mana Mana mucho worse for wear but buzzing from the overwhelming reception the Spanish had given us. They really know how to enjoy themselves and I was always surprised at their boundless energy when it came to partying. We got back to the hotel and crashed out before the long drive back to the ferry port and home , signalling the end of my first European Tour with Alien Sex Fiend.

Chilled on the beach for a few hours in the morning to recover from the gig. Caught some rays and even kicked a ball around before jumping in the tour bus and home.

" ADIOS AMIGOS " with. mucho regrets !!

CHAPTER THREE

Nightmare Zone

Back to Blighty after the scintillating experience of Spain; back to wind, rain, grey days but at least I was going home to see friends, family and Nicci, the woman I fell in love with, married, had a baby daughter with and eventually lost, but that was all to come. I just wanted to get home to the flat, chill and spend as much time with her as possible. Just isolate, masticate and fornicate after the tour. Nicci and I had been together since the first night I met her down in a club in Lytham. It was love at first sight; another of those feelings you just gotta" go with and I did. Nicci and I had some wild times; some tender times and some bad times. Okay, we didn't make it but she will always be with me in some form or another.

We locked ourselves away and indulged in eating, drinking and watching videos. Back to planet Earth for a while which I badly needed to do before life with the Fiends kicked off and Rat Fink would be at it once again. The second part of the tour was an interesting proposition; Scotland and London down for the business and real biggies they were going to be, especially the London gig because we'd be playing at home. That thought alone was freaking me out but it had to be done and I knew I was up for it.

Birmingham's Irish Centre was the venue for the next gig and I managed to grab a lift down with John Bentham, he was on his way down to video the night's events for a forthcoming release. Our kid Steve came along too with Richard King and Russ Casskev, the Joe Strummer of Lytham. Nik wasn't feeling up to his Fiendish self that evening; full of the flu but the show had to go on, especially as our Steve was with me and wanting to see his kid brother going through the motions. We did do a serious wig-removing version of Wild Women which John used on his video but halfway through It Lives Again, Nik looked thoroughly fucked - snot dribbling from his nose and walking around the stage with it dangling from

Nicci and Rat

his hooter and catching it with his tongue. Aaaarrrggghhh!!; real fuckin'' horror show stuff. We never needed special effects when Nik decided to go into one, flu or no flu.

Party time after the show with all concerned well pleased with the night's events. John was raving on about how much good footage he'd got and all the rest of it. John loved the Fiends and often turned up with his gear to shoot us; enthusiastic and funny with it as well as being extremely hardworking but not enough to stop him providing us with the occasional sidesplitter. We were in a hotel room in Manchester one night so John decides to film Nik in the shower and to do this effectively, had to contort himself into some very strange positions. Perched on top of a toilet seat, he settled down to film but blew it bigstyle; foot slipping into the loo and bringing down the shower curtain with him in an attempt to stop himself falling, but he ended up on his arse. So fuckin'' hilarious but at least the camera and footage were saved.

Our Steve was well knocked out with the gig and emotions were running high all around. Russ was well freaked out by it too and I was pleased they'd not only come to see me but had enjoyed the gig as things were hotting up. The roller coaster ride of a lifetime with the Fiends was about to begin as the London gig edged nearer which mean't I was going to have to be on top form and prove a point to the Fiend fans that I was the man for the job. We did Nottingham; Zhivagos and destroyed every music-loving arsehole in there. They were all stood around like a bunch of fuckin'' posers and Nottingham did not go down well with me at all. My card playing rapper mate Baron Puppet didn't accompany us to

Hold on ta ya hat Mr Fink

Europe but he was there on the second leg of the UK tour; they didn't like him in Nottingham and gave him loads of verbal shit. The arrogant bunch of bastards.

London next and my baptism of fire was drawing uncomfortably closer. The Astoria in Charing Cross Road was to be the venue and the preparations were well hectic the whole of the day; organising the promotional stuff and what have you. I remember standing in the middle of this huge great stage and thinking that this above all other shows, was to be the most significant of my life with the Fiends. The fans were turning out en masse tonight; coming to see the Fiends and check out the new drummer in the same process to see if he came near to Johnnie HaHa or not. The show was upon us and there were hundreds of kids locked outside the place before the doors finally opened to let them in. In they rushed like a gigantic swarm of demented killer bees in a scene very reminiscent of an Alfred Hitchcock movie. Showtime was just around the corner and was I shitting myself !!

I couldn't help thinking I had to prove myself out there tonight in front of the adoring army of fans. The atmosphere in the dressing room was very calm considering what lay ahead; the Fiends as a musical entity had to go out and prove themselves as a lot of heavy music journalists were in the audience and wanting a shitkicker of a show, so at least I wasn't the only one on trial. Suddenly Billy pops in with the dreaded announcement "ten minutes" and I started to flap bigstyle.

I stopped spliffing and swapped for Jack Daniels because I could feel my insides getting tighter and tighter. I poured out a large unhealthy cup of Jack and coke and steadied myself for combat. The walk down the stairs I will never forget as we were escorted by three hefty looking bouncers while the stairs seemed to go on forever and ever; like we were descending into the inferno itself. A world inhabited by fire, mutants, devils, demons and gargoyles. The chants from the waiting crowd grew louder and louder as we stood behind the huge black curtains. I was jumping around; up and down as high as I could and punching the air as well as diving into the side of the stage with a vengeance. "Right ! Come on. Let's sort this fuckin" lot out." Johnnie had gone and I was here so there was nothing to prove that I couldn't prove.

With that in mind we took the stage together like a conquering army ready to do battle one more time. The gig was fuckin" amazing; people jumping off the balcony and landing on just about anybody they fell on;

screaming injured people all around. Very reminiscent of the carnage in Paris but it was so often like that when the fiends did the business. Total self-destruction and nothing less was acceptable from King Nik.

Nik and Chris were pleased with the confidence oozing from every pore during the gig; we'd pulled it off knowing a lot of the music industry heads would be there watching; totally fuckin" their brains in with a relentless thumping unsurpassed onslaught of sound. No inhibitions or fears; we just squashed them into the ground that night. We'd come away with a result on home ground. Afterwards I was relieved that the whole thing was over and done with. Before heading up to Scotland, we chilled for a couple of days down in Brighton, much needed !! Went to the cinema. Checked out the local bars and just explored the place while coming down from the Astoria experience before Bonnie Scotland here we come.

Now this was going to be another mental experience. The scots have very warm hearts as far as the Fiends go even now and they knew how to party whenever we drove past Hadrians Wall to do the business. A couple of shows and the tour was over; sad really because I was getting into the way of life on the road but only a temporary blip on my map. Edinburgh's first stop with its' beautiful old buildings, Princes Street and the castle keeping an eye out over everything. The venue wasn't large by any means; a capacity of four hundred tops but even so, we were ready with all out claws sharpened ready for showtime.

I've never seen so many people pissed out of their heads under one roof. Fuckin" mental it was; whisky

The Fiend experience

bottles and staggering and falling all over the gaff. Wild drinkers each and every one of them. The dressing room was a tiny affair and every so often, in would burst a couple of crazies to wish us all the best; telling us we were fuckin" amazing and all the rest of it and that was just pre-showtime.

RIP was a monster fave among the folks past Hadrians Wall so Nik duly obliged, sending the crowd into a bloodcurdling highland frenzy. A wild gig that ended up with us being covered in beer and sweat. Something that night edged Nik into fits of temper; spinning his mike stand around through Buggin Me and ramming it into this bunch of blokes at the front of the stage, smacking one of them right in the kisser with it. "I don't like fuckin" Perrier water" he screamed while I was thinking let's get the fuck off the stage as they were well hard looking but as always, Nik took control and sorted it in his own inimitable way.

Aberdeen next up and what was to be my last gig with the Fiends for a while. I was going to miss the roadies too, the coolest bunch of jokers in the cosmos who'd made me laugh so many times throughout my initial gigs. They worked their fingers to the bone to provide Nik with the kind of stage setting and sound he insisted on

and that was every night too. The gig was scheduled in a huge hotel called The Victoria. Downstairs of which was a huge hall they reserved for functions and what have you. It wasn't that busy but all the same, we were our usual wired up selves to make sure the people were treated to a hell of a show. I didn't know it at the time but being the very last show of the tour, the roadies had planned something special for me that began with Moz escorting me to my drumkit as usual so I didn't trip up and go sprawling into the gear they'd worked so hard to set up.

As the smoke lifted I noticed I was missing my sticks. "Shit! Where the fuck can they be?" Not in the usual spot on top of the snare drum so I checked the case strapped to the floor and found them drowned in baby oil. Nice one but there was worse to come. I started playing and suddenly, fuckin" talcum powder everywhere; covering me from head to talon each time I banged the fuck out of my skins and the roadies in heaps of howling laughter at the side of the stage. It was my worst nightmare and did they come over and clean up their mess ? No fuckin" chance so I was left looking like the abominable snowman throughout the gig. Obscenities were shouted to one another but all in all the gig went well despite their warped sense of humour. Nice one lads !!

At the end of the gig, we all jumped on stage and announced it was the final show, giving one another a big hug for a job well done before adjourning for a beery binge up. The hotel owners kindly kept the bar open for us till around four in the morning so we could get pissed out of our tinies as we mumbled reminiscences over the past few weeks, and plenty of reference to the baby oil too suggesting I use that little number on Nicci on my return to leafy Lytham. "Yeah lads. Very funny".

We awoke the next morning feeling like death warmed up. The Fiends were heading back to London so I was getting a lift back home;telephoning my mum up and freaking her out with the news that the Fiends were calling round to meet her. She did me proud though with an impressive array of sandwiches and cakes for everyone, along with pots of boiling hot coffee. After a pleasant afternoon chinwagging, Mr and Mrs Fiend and the crew departed for Brighton; quite a sad parting but it had to be done. I knew there would be more stuff coming off with them in the future so it was chill out time again for yours truly.

Back to the reality of life in a small town where everything was painfully familiar but Nicci made it bearable. She'd landed herself with a new job, receptionist in an office dealing with buying houses so I decided to get a job to keep the boredom at bay. From being on tour and living through total insanity, I was now a hotel porter in Lytham. Talk about different. Sure it fucked me off but the money was needed to keep hold of the relationship with Nicci.

Meanwhile, I had the pleasant surprise of a close friend coming up to stay for the summer. Cherry who was from the States and a great muso came over for the summer of 87 and what a time that was. I managed to jump into a few sessions with my old musical buddies Russ Casskey and his band The Buggs were at it again and we played some wild gigs that summer; even getting a band together with Cherry and doing a show in The Winter Gardens in Blackpool.

Throughout that summer Nik and Chris remained in contact, keeping me wired of anything coming up; they'd discovered this great new recording studio in Surrey that went under the intriguing name of House in the Woods. Planned to go into the studio to record some fresh material for the new LP. During the session they'd met up with this cool sound engineer called Doc Milton and so they recorded stuff like Here Cum Germs, Isolation and My Brain Is In The Cupboard Above The Kitchen Sink. Shitkickin' titles and Nik was going into one about Doc and how sussed he was and the sound he produced being a veritable joy to their ears.

Nik suggested coming down to meet him which I did later that summer; one that ended with Cherry heading back to London leaving me feeling restless but my prayers were answered when Nik phoned me in August with the outrageous news that the Coops was down for an appearance headlining at Reading. Cool or what ? The Fiends being a bit chummy with Alice were invited to a private function at The Limelight Club and asked me if I would like to attend. Would I?? No fuckin' sweat as I ran around the flat like a headless chicken at the news I was going to meet one of

The one and only Cherry

All time great - Alice Cooper

supplied with lot's of fast whizz and Jack Daniels. Flattened two bottles and three wraps before heading off to the club and the whole thing about meeting Alice; not such a big deal for Nik and Chris as they'd met the man before, but for me, it was and still remains one of the highlights of my life. I was fucked but still managed to get my shit together before the cab arrived at the Limelight for the meeting. Falling out of the cab onto the pavement; it was so hilarious with all these muso knobheads waiting patiently to get into see the great man and there we were breezing past totally off our fuckin" noodles with VIP passes howling our heads off.

The club overdosed on darkness with loads of smoke-filled rooms but we eventually succeeded, slipping into the VIP room feeling like one of Alice's slithery pet snakes. The room was dark; full of corners and hideaways where you could get up to fornication and nostril business without detection but that night, it was best behaviour all round as we were ushered into a room crammed full of muso journalists and celebs waiting to meet Coops. Stood at the bar in a heap

my all-time heroes. The one and only Alice Cooper. Legged it to the store and bought the biggest bottle of wine I could carry; Nicci was so funny watching me go into one over this news. I stuck a load of his old tunes on; Black Juju, Sick Things, You Drive Me Nervous; Raped and Freezing; turned up the volume with a fuck the neighbours head on and went for it. Tough shit !

Jumped a train to Cardiff and met up with the Fiends before heading off to Yaxi's abode in London, well of dishevelled glory was John Hurt the Elephant Man himself. Completely off his tree and looking more like his screen character than he did in real life. The Bananarama girls were in there clutching their llittle cocktails as if their lives depended on it; Metallica were throwing verbal abuse out to all the bimbos without a care in the world while drinking gallons of beer. Mary from Gay Bikers On Acid was having a good old chinwag to Nik and Chris while Yaxi and yours truly were handing out flyers about the new soon to be released Fiends LP.

The two of us were having a right old laugh with that gravelly voiced legendary headbanger Lemmy from Motorhead; creeping over to us to take the total piss out of this tasty looking bit of leather skirt standing at the bar, wearing an ultra short, tight leather skirt. Lemmy subjected her to a verbal assault centering around the burning question she just would not answer. Namely, was she wearing any underwear or not? The poor girl ended up totally humiliated by the mad rocker; making rather a sharp exit with the question of underwear still unresolved. So much more intriguing to leave it there I think !!

The arrival of the Coops signalled a stampede from the muso journalists, all itching to get the first word in; the first piccie and what have you and it was a good half hour before he was finally free of them all so we chilled out at the bar watching all the grief until all the news-hungry leeches had departed the scene; following Nik and Chris over into this darkened corner of the room, there he was. The Coops himself looking regal, calm and collected as Nik introduced me to him.

I shook his hand and a brief conversation ensued. Such a quiet voice; noticeably diminutive in stature compared to his outrageous shock rocker blood and gore alter ego and I couldn't help noticing how small and cold his hand was; like shaking hands with a smooth-skinned friendly reptile. Very vampiric in his looks; dark eyes, pale skinned with a most unusual tone in his voice as he asked me how things were working out for the Fiendy's drummer as he liked to call them. He was knocked out by the news I was actually in the fanclub before graduating to the band. His wishing me the very best for my future signalling the end of a memorable meeting with the man I'd been in to since the year dot.

Party-time was beckoning us so we all adjourned to Browns to get into one. I was in such a great mood after the Coops experience and we all piled into this poor girls car wearing our serious party heads; crawling off to the party venue in search of drugs, sex and debauchery. The place was very upmarket, full of posers and assorted pop luminaries; there we were, a total contrast in our Fiendish guises having a riot as the looks of disgust and "who the fuck are this lot" reigned down from all sides. I remember taking the piss out of Elton John and George Michael as they sat at the bar with their adoring fans. The Fiends recorded a song called Boots On and there's a line in that song..."I don't wanna look like Elton John. Nice suit with my hair all gone." Nik and I couldn't help but crack up with laughter as the line flooded into our heads everytime we clocked him at the bar. Eventually burnt out and staggered back to Yaxi's abode around five in the morning thoroughly fucked.

It was early 88 and we were about to embark on a cosy tour around the UK. Yaxi was becoming more and more disgruntled with the band and Bradford was to be his last appearance with us and for me personally, that show proved to be the most demoralising of them all. The gig turned out to be a killer but Nik and Yax were at each others throats; towards the end of Boneshaker Baby, Yaxi went into one going completely fuckin'' mental. Smashing up everything in sight; guitars, amps, booting in the lights with his smelly plates of meat; it was one man fuckin'' chaos featuring a finale ending with him smashing his guitar all over the debris-littered stage and leaving, with the crowd thinking it was all part of the show.

Nik and Chris were gutted; the Fiends always ran on a shoestring budget with no room for luxuries like buying new equipment and there was Yaxi doing his best Tasmanian Devil number, smashing things up. The atmosphere in the dressing room was like a graveyard at midnight in January; Yaxi remained silent; not speaking to any of us and kept it like that the whole journey back to Brighton. He went on to London and got dropped off at his flat with the remains of his smashed up gear.

Major crisis for Nik and Chris sorting out all the budget for replacement gear while I was glad to get out of it for a few days and back home to peace and quiet. It's funny when I look back; I needed the chaos, the confusion and the insanity of touring. It was RatFink's blood transfusion when stocks were running low and they needed to be replenished with fresh thick life-sustaining blood but at times, it was so fantastic to just fuck RatFink off altogether and be myself. See Nicci and my family; fish and chips; a drink with friends; the pictures and just living in another

world, a galaxy removed from the chaos of Nik Fiend's domain - in so many ways the perfect addictive love hate relationship.

I arrived home and after giving Nicci the unbelievably bad news, settled into my relationship with her once again but still hoping things would be sorted out in an amicable way. A few months slipped by in which changes took place in both our lives. Nicci and I moved into a new flat and then came the news that was to change both our lives forever - a child was on the way and Nicci and I were to be parents !!

This had been planned because I really was into Nicci; the only woman who knew me both inside and out and the only one I truly wanted to be with. Sure, we had tons of the usual domestic shit to deal with like bills and all the other crap life deals you, but we had a deep underlying, understanding love for one another that pulled us through and with a baby on the way. Well, I was well pleased with life. The Fiends kept in contact and told me there was a major problem brewing with the record company insisting on a new LP and pretty quickly too. But Yaxi had left them high and dry so this looked like mission impossible and all around, the smell of trouble was in the air.

Right at the time they needed something to save their skins, up pops Doctor Milton. He played guitar as well as other multi-talented skills that filled the gap the Fiends needed filling perfectly. Along with another very handy guy called Kevin Armstrong, who as well as playing with top celebs like Iggy Pop, David Bowie and Paul McArtney, had produced some of the Fiend's earlier stuff. Nik and Chris gradually began to feel comfortable enough to sit down and pen some new material with these guys around them.

With Yaxi now out of the frame, there were holes to be filled to save HMS Alien Sex Fiend from going down to a watery grave. I'd spent a few weekends with them discussing the future over spliffs and mugs of tea knowing this was the most troubled period of their lives. Told them I could find my way around a guitar good enough to fill in for the missing Yaxi - a skill once again I have to thank our kid for teaching me at a younger age. Drum machines posed no problems to me either so with this previously unrequired versatility at my disposal, I began to fry Nik's bacon with it. Just messing around with the guitar and drums but he liked the "in ya face" attitude of my playing - chunky with a bit of boneyard buzz thrown in for good measure.

Nik and Chris told me all about the final meeting with Yaxi and the way he put it across to them confidently that without him, the Fiend's would be well and truly fucked. It was make or break time for them; for all of us concerned with the band. Yaxi's words lit up a fuse in me and I became determined not to let him have the last laugh; determined to prove Alien Sex Fiend were bigger and better than him. This belief came from two sides of my personality; the one time fan and now the musician and band member. I was on a mission to prove to Nik and Chris that we could go onto bigger and better things without him. Not just with the songs either but get the vibe back and turn it into something a lot more powerful to make sure that the starship Sex Fiend would once again blast off into the cosmos with or without Yaxi.

Nik and Chris were well into all my new found youthful energy and threw me in at the deep end to record

The saviour - Doc Milton

Nightmare Zone. Kev Armstrong did his bit but freaked himself out while doing a session recording Instant Kama Sutra; always heavily into his meditation was Kev and somehow he lost it and couldn't put himself back together enough to carry on with the Fiends. Doc Milton stayed on board though and struck up a really good friendship with Nik and Chris. I finally got to meet the man doing a session at Terminal in London. Stormed through a shit-hot version of Hawkwind's Silver Machine with yours truly doing guitar and backing vocals; hitting it off with the Doctor instantly.

We all got on like a house on fire and soon forgot who Yaxi was and then the good news. Nik and Chris were confident enough to venture out into the big wide world again as a four-piece band and do the business like we used to do it, if not better. The new LP was finished and the single Bun Ho was all set for release. Spirits were high in the Fiend camp as we looked forward to new hopes and ambitions with all this new artistic energy and direction. The LP was called Another Planet; unconventional in Alien Sex Fiend terms but still a good LP considering all the shit Nik and Chris were having to deal with at that low time in their musical development.

Chilling out in Cardiff for a few weeks at Nik and Chris's abode and having a few laughs along the way, Nik had met this cool guy called Frank who owned this wild club in Cardiff; the Square Club and we'd all spend our weekends in there getting totally shitfaced. I loved it and spent many late nights trying to get back to Fiend headquarters off my face. One night Nik and I were completely legless on our arrival back home. Chris was just stood there laughing at the pair of us, we were in such a state. Nik throws a serious spew all over the kitchen floor while I was feeling like my fuckin'' head was about to explode and there was Mrs Fiend laughing her head off.

We zipped through a number of warm up gigs to get back into the swing of things before showtime abroad. The Square Club was the venue and we treated the locals to some serious skullsnapping tunes before heading off on a combined UK and German tour. It was strange to swallow this time around; no Yax and me taking over his place in the band as drummer and guitarist. Simon who was now officially christened The Doctor, also played guitar during the time I drummed. We were a good double act and he would kick in some great riffs on the drum machine when it was my turn to get on the guitar; always slightly reticent during showtime; often hiding behind the monitors whereas with me, i loved it out there. Upfront where the monitors bled and the sound of chainsaw guitars; throbbing, grinding pulses, bass riffs and Nik's banshee screams ripping my ears apart.

After the warm up's were over and we were then ready to kick the arse out of the population once again, I had some time back home to see Nicci and find out how our unborn child was getting along. It was becoming increasingly difficult to leave her in what was her greatest time of need but she knew and understood the situation I was immersed in and went along with it. Besides the fact that I was doing what I'd always wanted to do, we both could see the potential successes to come out of Alien Sex Fiend and Nicci always filled me with the courage and determination to go out there one more time and have a go.

But even so, the partings were still very painful, especially now as she was pregnant and me not being there if anything untoward should happen. But, it was a case of doing what I had to do so we said our goodbye's and I headed back to Cardiff with my head full of all kinds of possibilities the new touring would bring in, but more importantly, the fact that I'd managed to prove Yaxi wrong and helped to put back together the band I cared about so much. We'd pulled through and were about to set out on a tour of shows that were spellbinding in every sense of the word. A chance to prove to ourselves and the fans that we were better than ever, with or without the rotting pong of Yaxi's feet under our noses.

CHAPTER FOUR

It Lives Again

Germany calling and the festival in Bonn where we were appearing with Lords Of The New Church. Over four thousand people packed in this massive concert hall that came with a hydraulic stage and a London double decker bus converted into a bar of all things. The Lords stormed through a blistering set and I remember thinking these are gonna be a tough one to follow.

As soon as the Lords finished , we were up next and no fuckin' about : straight into EST with the Doctor on guitar : the crowd went absolutely fuckin' mental and I switched instruments ; strapped on the guitar : a custom built Peavey with a top on off switch I loved messing around with and steamed straight into Smells Like Shit. The crowd was jumping around everywhere : up on stage and being thrown off only to climb back on to dive off once again into the seething mass of sweaty humanity going insane before us. At the end of the song Nik comes over : grabs me and said " told you it'd be alright Ratty. Now let's have a laugh ". Straight into Nightmare Zone. " They Even Took My Cat. . . Meeeeooooowwww !!. What a fuckin' night.

The fans screamed for encore after encore and the whole thing left a great taste in our mouths now the ghost of Yaxi had been finally laid to rest and had no chance to haunt the Starship Sex Fiend anymore. Nineteen eighty nine was going to be a wild year for me: Nik and Chris sorting out a nine date tour of Germany on the success of the record sales in that country.

The highlights of that tour were without a doubt Hamburg and Berlin : arriving in Hamburg we were greeted by these huge green and purple Sex Fiend posters everywhere. They looked the business and the gig was to be played in the Reeperbahn. The most famous redlight district in Europe. The venue was called The Docks : a huge affair with a really high stage area we could look down on the Fiend army from. The promoters were expecting around two to three thousand people and mobs of press and muso journalists turned up looking for after show interviews and piccies. Nik and I were painting up part of the stage set with loads of spray paint : red gloss everywhere that only freaked the venue owners out even more seeing us both hard at work.

Lot's of dripping smiley acid faces , skulls , voodoo and boneyard squiggles : faces painted on plyboard panels that fitted in front of

Be careful with that axe Rodent

the risers and when all was finished, everywhere looked very trippy and congratulated one another on a job well done. All the gigs in Germany were organised to perfection as you would expect from the Germans. We had to be on stage at either eight or nine o'clock prompt depending on which venues we were down for. As soon as the doors opened , in they came ; full within half an hour with an army of screaming demented crazies stamping their feet and calling for us to get our arses out on stage. " Sex Fiend. Sex Fiend ". The shouts were deafening even from the dressing room so we stuck on the ghetto blaster to chill out before showtime.

The gig was breathtakingly good from start to finish and we left the crowd screaming for more. Loads of people appeared backstage after the gig for the interviews , piccies and general handshaking and smiling ; all accompanied by chilled champers and spliffs. Headed off into the bowels of the redlight area afterwards in search of sex and cheeky bottoms. Loved the food over there too : the sausages were always a firm favourite with us all , especially the Currywursts. Wunderbah !!.

My first time in Berlin was truly memorable, with it's surreal very grand looking architecture and the famous Brandenburg Gate. The art capital of Germany full of smiling very stylish cosmopolitan people milling around everywhere : the gig was down for the popular Metropol Theatre where several years previous I visited. They filmed Dario Argento's " Demons " in the theatre so the gig held extra spice for me that night because that movie is still one of my all time favourites. We did a stormin' version of Get Into It, complete with flickering drum patterns throughout the song and Nik running all over the stage doing his usual demented self screaming " I am New To It From Another Planet. Get Into It ".

Nik was his brilliant best that night. Looking like one of the demons from the film : the way his

Fiendish goings-on in Lamberto Bava's Demons

make up had melted all down his face and the flood of bright green lighting adding another touch of swamplike horror to the show. I don't know but he looked fuckin' awesome, demonic going through his act. The Fiends were never short of a blisteringly loud PA system whenever we took Germany. It was just the way they liked it : thumping mindnumbingly loud and Faust and Elmar were the ones who always obliged us with the loudest gear possible with their monstrous rig of some twenty five k sound output. It was like thunder and lightning going off and such a shame our man Jim Lusted missed out twiddling the knobs on that tour as he would have loved it, but far too busy that time around.

Prior to the tour , Nik and Chris had chanced upon this guy : Len Davies who'd been working in a studio in Cardiff : seemed like a nice chap so got the job but he was always a bit too nice for my liking if you know what I mean. Fuck all compared to Mr Lusted but he wasn't available so Len took his seat on The Starship Sex Fiend for a couple of years. Strange kinda guy with a monstrous appetite. Forever stuffing himself with food and he liked his music very straight: Samantha Fox tunes if you can believe this and he would freak everybody out whenever he fancied a blast of her. Always eating and eating and eating !!

After Germany , it was home for a couple of weeks to friends and family but that was all : we were off once again touring the UK before heading out to Espania and The Fallus Festival once again. Eighty nine proved to be a busy busy year

for the Fiends and the new tours were called The Too Much Acid : appropriately named as it all turned out and such a great buzz to be back in Spain ; this time with a better stage set , excellent new songs and new people. Things were going well !

Many of the shows were recorded live during this hectic period and the record company were chasing for a new live LP and a double one at that. But there was no problem as we had some put down some great stuff on our crazy travels so after a chilling out period, Nik and Chris with the assistance of Doc Milton got down to some serious work : compiling the very best of all the shows and giving birth to their first live Sex Fiend LP since Liquid Head In Tokyo way back in nineteen eighty five. America was on the blower with offers to come and play out there as the word was spreading that the Fiends were quite a special audio visual theatrical horror show package.

They'd done the states back in eighty four with the original line up and the hunger they created in the fans never died. Thoughts of America now flooded my head. A place I'd always been into since watching Kojak , Starsky and Hutch, The Fonz and The Munsters.

Germany calling us once again though this time only for a quick two weeker ; all concerned raving about us after the recent shows we'd done there. But along with the good news there was some seriously shit news to deal with. A letter was sent to the record company : the German equivalent of the Anti Nazi League had sent it informing us that next time the

Fiends were appearing in Germany, then they were going to be done in. This was bad news as we had never been a band to indulge in the bullshit world of politics and suchlike stuff.

Turned out a fanzine was doing the rounds in Germany with a picture of Nik himself on the front complete with Adolf Hitler moustache and wearing a swastika on his tee shirt complete with a bubble coming from his mouth uttering some pro nazi words. Absolute bollocks, but death threat or no death threat we had to go : business was at the end of the day, business. Venues had been booked and tickets sold so there was no way out for us. Cancelling would have been disastrous for all concerned.

Paranoia was everywhere as we arrived in Frankfurt surrounded by some chunky looking bodyguards hired by the record company to keep us safe. Wolfgang was smiling from ear to ear as we appeared and I breathed a massive sigh of relief at the sight of these bodyguards : three of your typical huge blond German types in black bomber jackets : we were handed a can of CS gas each to carry with us at all times and instructions to terminate at the slightest hint of danger. Two of the bodyguards were men and the other a girl. All came tooled up with lot's of handy bone crunching, flesh ripping gadgets concealed about their persons ; their combined knowledge of the martial arts was phenomenal to say the least. It felt like we were in safe hands.

Even so, the thought of playing live to packed audiences knowing some mental fucker was out there was a tough one to deal. It was impossible to deal with the actions of a single nutter and all it would take was for somebody to pull out a shooter and start blasting away and it would be curtains for the Fiends. Bottles , coins and cans were always thrown at us during showtime : just a friendly natural reaction from the fans I guess but this was a whole new ball game to deal with. Even so , all the shows were sold out and everybody concerned seemed in good spirits that we were once again back on German soil but that initial ten minutes after going on stage was just a fuckin' nightmare , wondering what was going to happen.

Towards the end of the tour, we were down for playing a gig in Munster ; a great old hall with a host of carved figures strapped to the balcony and all very unusual. We were storming along at the usual pace when all of a sudden , a group of skins appeared, freaking loads of people out with their menacing appearance. Just stood their with their shaved heads seriously eyeballing everybody and putting down bad vibes. They started their act ; punching and kicking a few of the audience but Nik wasn't having any of it. Told me to stop playing and get the fuck off the stage. The skins throwing out a rain of verbal abuse and I got covered in what I thought was a pint of beer thrown from one of their mob.

WRONG !. Back at the dressing room , to my horror , I realised I was covered in piss as well as getting a serious cut under my eye caused by a sharpened up

Rat with Chryste Hall the Fiends Amercian tour manager

coin at me that could have all so easily taken my eye out. I jumped in the shower to sweeten up and returned with Nik Chris and Doc to finish off the gig. Back on stage, the skins were nowhere to be found leaving us to get on with the show. The tour ended successfully, thanks to Wolfgang and the chunky bodyguards who pulled us through with their crazy sense of humour.

America was looking good thanks to the Fiendish pair working like demented demons with Chryste Hall the American tour manager : dates being finalised , PA sorted and hotel bookings and all the other unseen complexities that go into a tour. Throughout the summer we kept in close contact, while in the meantime , Nicci gave birth to an eight pound seven ounce beautiful baby girl : Kashia Cherry with her bright beaming eyes staring out at me as I held her for the first time, completely shellshocked over the fact I was now a father.

Nicci remained in hospital overnight so I headed back to the flat meeting up with her sisters boyfriend to crack open the champers and celebrate Kashia's birth. Things eventually settled down and the three of us moved into a more spacious flat in St Annes : above a chippy too which was very handy as the owner often treated us to free fish and chips but the time was ticking by and I only had a couple of precious months to spend with my family before heading off to the states and the pinnacle of my life with the Fiends.

With visas and passports sorted , I said my tearfilled goodbyes to Nicci and Kashia before hopping on the Cardiff train to meet the team : they were all waiting, raring to go. Most of our gear was being hired in the States to cut down on all the problems connected with such things : I was pleased at the news. The flight was around six hours in all , during which we all had a right old laugh playing stupid games and getting off our faces. The hostesses were freaking out and couldn't believe our sense of humour but it was all done in the best possible taste with no harm intended. They loved it really but it was more than their job was worth to join in with us all.

We finally landed on the tarmac at Boston where the weather was pleasantly warm with the air being laced with the smell of gasoline hanging around. We were all met by Chryste and Beth, the advanced publicist on the tour. We were ushered onto a spacy looking tour bus feeling like proper popstars. We were down for the East Coast and an appearance in New York which pleased me no end as it was one of those places I'd dreamed of visiting.

It was The Too Much Acid

Tour to coincide with the release of the new live LP which was selling well stateside : our spirits were high and we were ready to kick some good old USA ass. Chryste's Ma and Pa had planned a very agreeable welcoming for the Fiends: walking into a huge American banquet that filled us all up. Chryste sorted us out with a million useful tips , maps , badges , stickers and all kind of boneyard things. Halloween was just around the corner and we all got well stoned on some seriously headdoing grass: taking my head off in the process so much so that I had to do a sharp exit for a short time to get my shit together ; sitting in the garage to chill out and make sure it was still connected to my neck before going in for more.

Chryste really gave her all whenever the Fiends appeared on her doorstep ready to tour and helped us all out in every way imaginable. One night after our arrival , Nik decides on a complete set change and once again his artistic creativity shined through by turning a couple of hundred dollars worth of rubbish into stage effects in the way only he could. It was fuckin' freezing that night but we were all in the garage working our knobs off for foreman Nik. It was a case of tea break over lads as myself , Andy , Moz , Paul , Chryste and a couple of friends all set about constructing the stage set.

Nik changed the cell block door : covered it in skulls and the poor old mannequins got the full major surgery treatment too. We swallowed gallons of steaming hot coffee and smoked spliffs as we worked to help keep the cold away

Rat and Nik Fiend in New York

from our sore fingers. Some pop stars we turned out to be working like a bunch of self employed builders constructing our own stage set ; not exactly how I imagined it would be but then again , that's how life was a lot of the time with the Fiends. Different and with plenty of variety to keep you on your claws.

We were all thoroughly jet lagged the following day so it was time to catch up on the lost zzz's before setting out to do the business. We did so many shows in the States and most of the time, it felt like we were drowning yesterday. The first gig was at a club was called the El N Gee : inside was this huge helicopter which housed the mixing desk for the stage show and these wild trippy toilets all sprayed up fluorescent paint. The gig was completely fuckin' mad considering it was a small place in comparison to some of the German venues but so fuckin' what : the crowd loved us and we loved them. It was good to be playing in America.

New York was breathtaking in every way imaginable. the Big Apple : Broadway : Times Square.

Like a set from Superman or Batman. The gig was at a club called The Limelight : a building a statement in itself like something out of one of those classic gothic Hammer horror films : a huge church with wrought iron railings round the perimeter and these grass bits that gave the appearance of a graveyard. We were made to measure for The Limelight Club.

The interior was something else too : the original pews had been removed and in their place , a dancefloor with an altar being the stage. I mean ; what more could we want from a venue !. These huge speaker systems erected directly in front of the stage and above , strapped to the ceiling were these human figurines in unimaginable positions. Interesting secretive bars with the barstaff in skimpy clothing looking delectably fuckable and hot to trot. Male and female dancers in clear boxes : holes drilled in the boxes with these pervy rubber gloves connected to them : see a dancer you like and all you had to do was simply slip your hands into a pair of the rubber gloves and touch up the dancer of your choice

while they performed their sexy gyrations in time to the music in front of you. What a place !

The stage set was at it's finest that night ; draped in all the Sex Fiend muslin webs , freshly painted panels and dustbins full if skulls. Very twilight zone and with MTV there to film us at work, our spirits were high. Back in the dressing room , time was drawing nearer but we were all looking forward to the show. An old friend of the Fiendish couple turned up : Jolly who used to sell those famous punk badges wayback when. He was well pleased to see his old friends and proceeded to roll up a fearsome looking rug to celebrate their return to America.

Nik and I were soon in a state of complete hysterics after pulling off a few tokes from the joint and then it happened !. This weird feeling crawling up my back to my neck and shoulders and this banging in my head. I was howling with laughter when I realised what I was sitting on. Pulling back this huge tarpaulin to reveal an assortment of blocks of turf for the graveyard outside the church. Fell off rolling around in further hysterics as showtime crept nearer and nearer the appointed hour. Poor old Nik had to shoot off for another i n t e r v i e w : something I couldn't have done feeling

Ready to kick ass outside The Limelight

that stoned after doing some of the

strongest skunkweed going ; so Jolly said and I wasn't arguing with him.

The New York gig was Nik's Royale with cheese as that night he actually premiered his collection of artwork entitled The Diary Of A Lunatic before showtime. Nik has always been brilliant at art and for much of the day he worked hard fixing up his paintings so they could look the business and they did too. The whole place was simmering with anticipation that the Fiends were about to take the stage : like the witches cauldron out of Macbeth. Hubble bubble toil and trouble and all that. Showtime kicked off with It Lives Again and immediately the whole fuckin' place goes into warp factor.

We didn't give them time to bleed and ripped straight into RIP : we had a brand new arsenal of material to hit them with and they loved the new Fiends. New members and bigger and better than they ever were. We did a blistering set of songs with Nik producing the inflatable big yellow banana for Sample My Sausage. From the off Nik was brilliant. Had the crowd not only eating out of his hand but licking in between his fingers in the bargain. After the gig , we drove back to Boston, all concerned looking forward to the next show.

New York was special to me because I got to meet a personal legend from my childhood as I sat round the box goggle eyed watching the Munsters. After a spot of shopping and sightseeing , we were taken to a restaurant on Bleeker Street by the two Sandras from B-Side magazine. A restaurant owned by none other than Grandpa Munster himself Mr Al Lewis. There

he was done up in all his vampire costume and looking the bollocks and after friendly handshakes and words were exchanged between us all , out came the cameras and we had a few piccies taken with him. A brilliant finale to my introduction to The Big Apple. The food was pretty shit hot too : Italian and funnily enough , stuffed with garlic !

Next up, a club in Boston. A small place packed with party people ready to bop. It was Halloween too which is a big thing stateside. They really do go to town from the most grown up adults down to the smallest kid. The stage was done out to extra ghoulish proportions in celebration of the special night. Loads of pumpkins , hanging skeletons , bats and witches hats. The venue was called The Ground Zero At Manray and the tickets had been sold out well in advance so we were looking forward to a special show.

We walked out to an audience of decomposed rotting bodies , skeletons , werewolves , vampires , zombies : it looked like the entire cast from Dawn Of The Dead had turned out to pay homage to us. There were this one particular couple both dressed in wedding outfits leaping around to the sound of my twanging boneyard guitar and the whole scene was just very bizarre but pleasing to see so many people turning out with so much effort. Something they just couldn't be arsed doing over here. We all came away from Boston well pleased that the Fiends had managed to put on a cool show for the passionate crowd of fans.

Nik went one step further in a typically brilliant spontaneous

piece of showmanship that illustrated his comic genius to a tee: deciding to take to the stage wearing this fuckin' ginormous hollowed out pumpkin on his head. It was so heavy that a couple of the lads had to help him on with it. I don't know to this day how he managed to get through the show as he couldn't see a fuckin' thing but that apart , it looked awesome and really did the crowds heads in. Mr Pumpkinhead stole the show once again with his inbuilt very English manic artistic creative streak and the crowd loved it that night.

Cleveland Ohio was our next port of call, and a twelve hour overnight journey that brought home to me the vastness of America. The tour bus made up for it though with this wicked sound system and it felt we were on board a spaceship everytime we boarded that bus. Len drove and poor old Moz , Andy and Paul had to contend with his CB radio bullshit the whole time and listening to his hair wrenching music. Very strange guy that Lenny was. Finally hit Cleveland and straight into a fine example of a nationwide chain of hotels called the Days Inn Hotel. We renamed them to Days In Hell because there were some seriously bad shitholes but we coped.

Don't recall too much about the gig but I do remember Wolfgangs mate Roger turning up on this huge Harley D and a pocketful of spliffs to smoke so smoke 'em we did. The next show was much more of an eye opener : Detroit and the home of Motown , Iggy Pop , Alice Cooper and MC5. A city with a vast influential and credible musical heritage and here we were about to do the business in the Wolverine State although we weren't the ones on the menu. The gig was in the St Andrews Hall situated in a well dodgy part of town and freezing cold with it. The owners appeared with this weird looking heater that resembled something like an aircraft engine but it kept us all warm. On an old piano in the corner , Doc suddenly supplies us all with a rendition of Alice Coopers I Love The Dead. It sounded awesome and echoed all around the high ceilinged room leaving us all wide mouthed and shocked at his tricky finger skills.

Nik had told me that from his last experience playing Detroit that the crowd really were fuckin' mental, so we had to do the business like never before to keep them on their toes. The set was changed slightly : more of an attack edge to it to keep them there with us. To get to the backstage area we had to wait until everybody was in the venue. Then sneak out and go underneath this weird fuckin' club full of strange looking mothers. We took to the stage to thunderous applause and opened up straight away with Boneshaker Baby : the ultimate sucker punch. The place crammed full of Punks , Mohicans , Rockabillies , Hells Angels , Goths , Skins.

Chris and I were having a right old laugh together with our impromptu duet on guitars. " I am a boneshaker baby. Got this rattling in my neck ". A great gig and after evicting a mob of severely pissed off cockroaches from our hotel room we all set off for Chicago and another shitkicker of a journey. Chicago : smoke rising from the streets , classic old buildings , and the home of the infamous Al Capone and his gangster army. The venue we were due to appear in was the famous Cabaret Metro ; one of Chicagos top spots. Strangely disturbing from my point of view because of the fact they were showing stomach churning scenes of violence from the big video screens hung up on the walls to the grinding sounds of industrial music. Animals being tortured and killed , decapitations , autopsies : all in all, a disgusting spectacle watching the crowd getting off on all this blood and gore.

The gig was a fantastic affair, full to bursting with a lot of press and music people turning up to interview us and grab a quick piccie. While I was on the road , I managed to get my leather jacket sprayed up by this cool artist called Darryl. I liked Darryl and got stoned with him a few times. He was magic and well into hip hop art form stuff. As a special favour he produced this really cool looking colourful zombie on the back of my leather for me. Even sprayed up some special treats for the stage shows with an awesome assortment of skull and crossbone squiggles.

After Cincinatti , Pittsburgh and Atlanta , we finally hit the sunshine state of Florida. The travelling was doing me in but the sunshine and warmth recharged my emotional batteries bringing back so many vivid memories of Spain. Arduously long road journeys were a thing you just had to accept and get on with ; part and parcel of touring that vast expanse but it was something we could have all done without.

Mrs. Fiend in Chicago during the first US tour

Many times amid the commotion of Lens crazy headdoing music and numerous joints to help numb the boredom of impossibly long journeys , I often slipped into one and reflected back over the events of how all this crazy lifestyle came about. The local band scene in Lytham. John Bentham telling me to keep cool and go for it. The Turnpikes and our kid Steve pushing me into things he knew I wanted to be in. Memories of watching him on stage with the Zanti Misfitz ; the local bunch of rock n roll heroes he played with who almost made it.

He looked so fuckin' cool on stage and I always wanted to be like him , and there I was in this cosmic bus travelling to all parts of the States , very much a product of his interest and influence in my life. That cold van drive down to London with Ross Bowman stuck in my mind constantly. Him turning up at my house to take me down to the Fiends abode. The phonecall from nik telling me I was getting picked up and to pack my gear ready for the off. Trying to keep warm during the journey and all the time wondering what the fuck lay ahead of me : would I be good enough to pull it off ?. Would the Fiendish couple like me ?. And there I was touring the States with them ; all my questions answered in the best way I could think of. Fuckin' wild !!.

The gig was scheduled at none other than Mr Pete Stringfellows nightclub Who's In The Grove, situated in a high class shopping mall full of wealthy straights. To get to the club , a lift had to be used : all the gear for the show had to be packed on the lift and shunted up to be set up. A task the roadies hated with a vengeance but it had to be done. The club held around the three hundred mark and ticket sales were around the four hundred so already, trouble loomed but we got on with all the pre show shit regardless.

The terribly posh stuck up people in the shopping mall were freaking out at the sight of the queue of deranged crazies waiting to be let in as showtime drew nearer. We made a dash for it through the mall to a different lift to take us up to the venue. We all got in , closed the door , pressed the required buttons and lifted off. First floor , second floor and then bang !!. It happened. The lift jammed between the third and fourth floors with us in it. After the initial gut wrenching laughter had subsided , panic set in between us as we realised showtime was knocking on the door and we weren't answering.

So there we were going into one with Len doing his utmost to calm us all down. Nik was so funny and told Len to keep his trap shut; lit up a spliff and decided to get stoned while we waited for the arrival of International Rescue. In the meantime , chaos reigned supreme upstairs in the club as the roadies and management panicked at the disturbing lack of Sex Fiends in the building. Around fifteen minutes elapsed before somebody twigged that the lifts safety lock was in operation : another bang followed and there we were on our way to the stage looking well relieved that the show was going to be saved.

The club was tiny with the whole crowd virtually lying on top of us for the whole gig. Blistering hot too and Nik's perfectly applied make up only lasted about three songs before it began to melt down his face. The manager ended up getting the sack after the gig for not doing his research thoroughly enough. I think he was under the illusion that we were some kind of dance act or strippers, and we freaked him out when the realisation dawned on him we were exactly the opposite.

After Who's In The Grove, we headed for Orlando. The former home of the Seminole Indians who were slaughtered by both Spanish and English plunderers. I have always loved all aspects of the Indian cultures and to see it for myself was both enlightening and saddening to discover this once great people were slaughtered en masse and put out to graze on sub standard reservations to live out the rest of their days ; a once proud but defeated nation unable to live the way they had lived for generations.

The show was scheduled for The Beecham Theatre ; situated on a cool looking street full of pastel coloured buildings. The sun was out and the promoter and staff gave us

A quiet moment on the road during the first US tour

a warm welcome. The gig was a thoroughly enjoyable experience and we left Orlando in high spirits, as we travelled to the last gig in Tampa. The Bay Rowdies, the fabulous Busch Gardens, home to a myriad of exotically colourful animals and birds. The orange blossom and the sabal palmetto trees can be found growing in abundance.

This journey turned into a total fuckin" disaster as the truck carrying all the gear had broken down, so this mean't we had to move all the heavy stuff from the truck and dump it onto the side of the freeway so the wheel could be changed. We were already one hour late and still nowhere near the fuckin" venue ! Chryste took the decision to press on with the band to get to the club to save face so we left the roadies to sort out the shit. There were loads of people outside the Club Masquerade as we pulled up, thoroughly soaked from the torrential downpour that felt like it was drowning Tampa. The lads finally showed with all the gear totally pissed off and wanting to get on with it..

In a whirlwind of activity and grunting and swearing, we all jumped in and set up the gear. The club owners finally opened up the doors and let the army of drowned rats into the venue and we finished off the day with a great

gig; completely off our faces and even managed to dredge up a few laughs about the days unforseen stressful events before saying goodbye to Tampa.

My first American tour with the Fiends had almost come to its' conclusion but not before another ten hour journey to Charlotte in North Carolina and a club called The Pterodactyl. A great venue to play in and full of paintings of Dinosaurs. It also harboured a seriously shit-kickin' PA system for which we were all very thankful. After Charlotte, a soul destroying twelve hour marathon to Philadelphia which didn't do any of us the slightest bit of good.

Philadelphia couldn't handle us. We faced an audience of dumbstruck trendies with wide-open mouths who were in turn thinking "now just what the fuck is going on here then?" Nik just laid into them all the more; completely fucking up their heads with his incisive cockney, deadpan, chaotic brand of humour, leaving the expressionless, faceless bastards for dead. Next up Washington DC and The Nine Thirty Club where so many illustrious bands had played; The Cramps, Hawkwind and Nirvana to name but three and I was thrilled, walking out onto a stage knowing that some of the world's greats had been there before me.

The whole place crammed full of people wanting a seriously mindbending experience, so we kicked off with It Lives Again but had to call it a day halfway through, due to chaos going off all around us. There were echoes of Paris as i watched bodies flying all over the place. Pogoing, treading on each other, treading on all the gear and going fuckin" bananas with it. I lost sight of old Nik in among the screaming madness of the crowd. The security lost it for a few minutes amid the chaos and I remember ending up on the deck still hanging onto my guitar and trying to play.

Feet trampling all over me and my axe; getting kicked to fuck but as bad as it felt, the vibe was in no way a violent one. Just a chaotic totally mad, all consuming enjoyment if that makes sense ! The security guys eventually got their shit together, opened up all the fire exits and slowly cleared the stage of all the bodies and debris to enable us to proceed with the show. After sorting our shit out, we were up and running once again and piledrived them into the ground with fuckin" great versions of Smells Like Shit and Ignore The Machine to bring to a close a truly memorable gig full of all the feelings of euphoria that such an experience leaves you with.

I loved it all because to me, that is what the whole fuckin" thing was about; to be playing in a truly awesome band full of characters joined together to do the business in a thoroughly unique mindbending way. I loved the buzz of showtime when Nik's monster came to life; when the Alien Sex Fiend pulsed with a ferocious all-consuming energy that crushed the life out of anybody who got under its claws. Better than drugs, sex, Yorkshire tea, better than anything ! That buzz of being out there, vulnerable but at the same time in complete control. Both ends of the emotional scale. That's what it was all about to me and I loved every second of it.

Onto the final date of the US tour in New Jersey and a very odd gig to end such an unforgettable tour with. The venue being a restaurant of all places, stuffed full of people filling their faces with food and drink. We had to go on stage when all the diners had ceased their chomping activities. I wanted to go on while they were at it and give them something to make the fuckers puke up on but it wasn't to be. The gig was quite a boring affair to say the least, but by then, all I wanted to do was to get the fuck out of it and back to the comfort of home and Nicci and Kashia. I was drained and in need of some rest but it had been a fantastic time from start to finish.

I will never ever forget that first American tour with the Fiends. It's like anything that's enjoyable. The more you have the more you want, and in between times, it all gets too much and you just want out but you don't. You just go on and on and on until it's over, knowing you have had such a fuckin" riot along the way. And riot is a word that always springs to mind whenever I flashback to that mad crazy, but mindbendingly addictive first US tour.

We all exchange handshakes, hugs, goodbyes and see you again with Chryste and all the other good people who'd worked their arses off in putting together the tour for us. The gear was packed away for the last time and with tear-filled eyes, we boarded the plane back to the reality of life back in the UK once again. Boo Hoo !!

CHAPTER FIVE

Blessings of the State

It was great to be home with the family, telling them all about my American jollities. Having the chance to relax : get to know Kashia and Nicci again but I'd hardly come down off the tour when Cherry, a dear friend from the states appeared with a smile and a pocket full of nostril business. Good timing too from him as Nicci and I finally decided to tie the knot. After a reception , we all headed back to the flat for some serious food and drink : while the respective families were busy stuffing themselves into oblivion , Cherry and I hopped around to the nostril business, trying to keep the smile on Kashia's face.

Alice Cooper was back in the UK touring after the success of Poison : and scheduled to kick arse in Birmingham and Wembley. Nik Chris and I were down as guests at the Birmingham show ; thanks to the friendly assistant manager Brian Nelson. After a shitkicker of a show, we piled backstage to meet the Coops, as ever, surrounded by an army of press. He suddenly appeared wearing this awesome black leather jacket with a huge Black Widow spider on the back. I tried to swap my Zombiefied jacket for his but he wasn't having any of it. Well pleased to see us all though: wished him all the best and left him to it.

Christmas was upon us once again and Kashia's first. We had a great time of things despite Nicci being full of flu the whole time. Nik gave me the news that we were booked into The House In The Woods to record a brand new LP. I always looked forward to a session in that studio : met loads of friendly people and had some great times along the way getting off our faces. We did Zombiefied in the space of a couple of months and the new LP called Curse which came from a painting of Nik's. On the domestic front , we had the good fortune to move into a house owned by some friends who were on a move to Madrid. The house was just what we needed with a back garden for Kashia to run around in and a bedroom of her own. Life was full of everything to look forward too.

The next live show took place in Yugoslavia : a beautiful place called Pula situated on the Adriatic at a festival held in some football stadium. We were the headline band and what a completely mental weekend that was. Arrived at the stadium to be greeted by loads of smiling faces and this fuckin' ginormous eighty k sound system. It was boiling the whole time we soundchecked : hot enough to melt the leads and scores of people fainting under the blazing hot sun : the survivors drinking gallons upon gallons of water to keep them cool. Ian , an old mate of mine who played with me back on the local bandscene turned up with his girlfriend and we all had a good time chilling and reminiscing. As we were swamped out with work, Nik agreed to Ian jumping in to sort out the tee shirts and badges for us.

The people were making quite a fuss of us ; asking for autographs and piccies which was a nice welcoming gesture but on my return to the dressing room , I got an unexpected bollocking from Nik about indulging in such things. " We'll have none of that business Ratty " . We took the stage around three in the morning ; twenty five thousand packed into the stadium with campfires lit everywhere and the intoxicating smell of marijuana in the air to see us through. Showtime lasted some two hours before we called it a morning and shot off back to our hotel for some well earned zzzz's.

Woke up to glorious sunshine and a look around this friendly place we found ourselves in. Loads of people were rock diving into crystal clear water but we just watched the sights of people enjoying themselves as we had a busy time ahead of us after a break back in England : headlining a festival in Germany for late September in Hannover called The Festival Of Darkness. Sounded right up our street, with a whole host of goth bands appearing. The event was cloaked in darkness so for a change, the Fiends did it ultra clean with loads of powerful lighting on the stage with Nik going on in a white boilersuit splattered with fluorescent colours. He looked awesome in his whiter than white Mr Colgate image. A total contrast to all the other black and white doom and gloom goth bands but that was the beauty of Nik ; always possessing the ability to go against the expected grain.

That show was a serious turning point for us as a band in Germany. Our records were selling like brockwursts and the promise of more tours coming up in the near future. It was all becoming very hectic but that's what it was all about at the end of the day. Recognition by the fans , the promoters and the record company. The Curse LP was selling

Ain't got time to bleed in Yugoslavia

particularly well in the states so we were given the good news that there was to be a two month promotional tour that would take in the West Coast this time around. The city of the Lost Angels, Hollywood , sun and spiritual freedom. I couldn't wait.

We were down for playing Canada : Quebec and Montreal and the venue Foufones Electriques : the gig turned out to be a violent affair with loads of fighting going off all around us. One guy jumped up on stage and stuck his hands around my neck so I butted him off me : took off my guitar and then laid into him goodstyle. Meanwhile, Andy and Moz decided to jump in and threw the guy down the stairs, as things were slowly getting out of control. After showtime was over we were informed by the bunch of local rock n roll heroes called Voivoid that fighting was a genuine sign of appreciation in Montreal. The better the gig , the more violent it became: very odd.

Minneapolis up next and the home of Prince. The gig was to be at 7th Street Entry, the actual club where they filmed Purple Rain. A totally cool club sexy girls everywhere we looked. The snow was thick on the ground which made things very tricky indeed for all the crew in getting the gear in the club and set up on stage. All good fun being a roadie when the Fiends took to the road.

Kansas City up next and what a fuckin' place that was. The place was full of chemical factories belching out their shit and it had the smell of a million rotting corpses hanging in the air and dodgy looking ghettos you just wouldn't want to get lost in. The best thing I recall about the Kansas City experience was the ice cream bar next to the venue. The gig was okay but nothing special. Now the next one was special !. Denver Colorado in this little club called The Garage and they weren't wrong either when they called it that.

Literally a garage on the edge of this dodgy looking industrial estate but coming with a reputation as the hottest spot in town. And true to it's reputation , the kids were going completely fuckin' mental waiting for the Fiends to come to town for year and here we were to deliver their wish. The DJ was spinning a load of Ska music which I found well weird but there you go. Madness , Selector , Specials , The Beat ; the whole fuckin' club was kicking off to the sounds of Two Tone like you'd never imagine. It was as if we'd landed in the twilight zone and the last thing I expected to hear that night.

The gig was one of those unforgettable classics with Nik doing the whole show standing on a dustbin no less : bodies all over the

fuckin' place and would they let us get off stage. We'd taken our time coming to Denver and they were determined to drain every last drop of blood from our veins but we didn't give a fuck. It was such a buzz to be in front of a mad enthusiastic audience and we played for three sweat soaked hours and still they howled for more. They swamped the dressing room and later on , the tour bus climbing all over the bus like a load of deranged zombies ; even running after us as we shut the doors and pulled out of one of the best Fiend gigs ever. Goodnight Denver !

Denver to San Francisco next, which took in the region of twenty hours. One thousand two hundred and twenty six miles of road to digest as we travelled through the breathtaking lunar-like landscape of the Colorado desert. Mountain sides , rock faces and colours splattered everywhere like dripping paint. We finally hit San Francisco much to everyones relief as we motored over the Golden Gate bridge which was another one of those experiences. " And to the right of us ladies and gentlemen !. You will please note the island penitentiary of Alcatraz. Home of the Bird Man and Al Capone ". It was great to be in California and another dream come true after hearing so much about it from Cherry.

The DNA Lounge was our port of call. A funky club in downtown Frisco where all of Fat Freddys cats hang out : very pornographic and the kinda place that suited me down to the ground. The audience were a totally outrageous bunch of freaks. All of them done up in rubber and leather bondage gear , chain mail , and various other pervy attire. You name your perversion and it was in that club for sure. Very nice !. We took the stage and immediately the crowd went into one like they were having sex with one another. The whole club stank of the smell of sex and they didn't give a fuck that night. There were guys slipping fingers into womens orifices while they jumped up and down to our tribal beats and women giving guys hard on's in return. Cherry never mentioned anything like this in his LA stories and that was one night I would have much rather been watching than playing in the Fiends.

Hollywood was just as wild as I'd expected it to be ; pink poodles and silicone tits everywhere. Cherry had told me some great stories about the place and also , just how dangerous it can be to strangers if you didn't know where you were heading for. Our hotel was just around the corner to the famous Chinese Theatre where all the stars leave their handprints but sadly, there was no room for our clawmarks anywhere along the pavement !

We were taken to meet the promoter Bruce who was as cool as we'd expected him to be. Off shopping after friendlies were exchanged to record stores and some instore signings along the way. The show had been sold out for months and we were all well pleased at the news. After signings and handshakes, we shot off for a spot more shopping. Tee shirts , masks and all kinds of boneyard shit. The shops were another world. Crammed full of horror movie stuff that you hadn't a chance of getting

back in England.

The show was at The Helter Skelter on Sunset Boulevard. The club held around two thousand people : very low ceiling with a dodgy looking stage area nestled in the corner with guys nailing bits of timber to provide a makeshift security barrier between them and us should it all go mental. After soundchecking in , we headed back to the hotel to chill and get our shit together for showtime. Nearer the time we were getting reports that the place was jam packed to the rafters : hundreds of them causing trouble along Sunset Boulevard with the cops turning up and everything turning nasty. We arrived in the middle of it. Got off the bus and made a break for it.

We'd freaked the whole of the hotel staff out with our Fiendish appearance ; me in these Arnie style shades and feeling ready to terminate at a seconds notice. Down the lobby some bright spark shouted to Nik that he looked remarkably like Bette Davis when she was going through her Baby Jane period. Nik took it as a bit of a compliment and did a u turn with one of his cheeky smiles. We finally arrived at the club and were greeted by these stressed out security guards and a very irate club owner who was freaking out at all the commotion going off around his little empire. We hit the stage to complete fuckin' chaos with Nik deciding to open up with Zombiefied.

Whatever we opened with that night would have done the trick. They were fuckin' mental and once again , the whole thing felt and looked like Paris. I was up on a drum raiser so had a good view of

More mayhem from Alice

were being lifted across the stage area as the security guys attempted to clear the area of people and restore some semblance of order at the same time. They actually formed the barrier for the remainder of the show ; linking arms together and standing directly in front of us as we took to the stage for part two. Straight into EST Trip To The Moon as the crowd settled down and got into the show. The gig eventually came to a close, and we left the club in one piece. A lot of cool peeps had turned out that night including Alice Coopers main man Brian Nelson. We were up for hours yakking away while the Doc crashed out upright in this armchair looking hilarious.

everything going on around me. As Zombiefied reached it's peak , the barrier collapsed and it was case of here we fuckin' go. These poor kids were getting crushed against this shitty excuse for a safety barrier : the show was stopped to give everybody a chance to get their shit together before we kicked off once again. It was like Towering Inferno and Twister all in one and just another typical example of the frenetic chaos we filled our audiences with. It's a miracle nobody got killed at any of our gigs because so many ended up the same way. The UK , Europe and now the States.

All these pieces of timber

We had one more downtown LA show to complete. The venue itself was a Chinese restaurant of all things ; that night being neatly converted into a makeshift club with the speciality of the night served up in abundance. Fiend Chow Mein and Wok fulls of it. They'd even rechristened the place for the evening ; The Obituary and quite an appropriate title remembering the last gig, The dressing room was a complete fuckin' disaster and the kitchen was infested by the biggest motherfucker cockroaches ever seen: in between getting ready, we spent a large amount of time stamping on the big black shiny fuckers. Just like the cocaine bugs out of Cronenberg's Naked Lunch.

The gig didn't turn out to be as chaotic as the Helter Skelter but still lot's of energy bouncing around the place and a good time was had by all including a couple of guys from The Motley Crew who had their wigs seriously removed by another Fiendish musical and visual extravaganza. We finally said our goodbyes to LA and to all the great people who'd helped put the shows together : thanked all the hotel staff for their hospitality and that was us out of it and onto San Diego in the cosmic bus.

The Baccahnal Club was where we were headed for as we journeyed through strange lands complete with even stranger signposts proclaiming things like " Dustclouds For 11 Miles " and " End Of The Pedestrian Accident Area ". All very weird but San Diego was like that and reminded me a lot of Spain with similar architecture and vibes. We drove passed these two concrete domes and Nik was going on about them looking like a pair of ginormous tits sticking up out of the ground. There was shock with Andy as he came down with a nasty bout of food poisoning and had to shoot off to the hospital for treatment while the Doc battled away on stage with his guitar strings snapped. Still they all loved us down in San Diego despite that.

We were close to Mexico which meant hot weather and even hotter food for all concerned. Can't recall too much about the show but it took place in some kind of college campus and that's about it. The heat was rising as we hit Arizona ; where the Coops lives with his family and a state steeped in Indian culture. We visited several Indian reservations from the Papago and Hopi indians. What skilled crafts people they were especially in the exquisitely detailed working of silver and turquoise ; something they learned from the Mexicans in the early eighteen hundreds.

Tempe was to be our Arizona gig and the club was a small affair with loads of cool hippy types hanging around with copious amounts of spliffidge upon their persons. I remember Can being played through the PA as we pulled up and the whole was very relaxing. Before the gig we even got through to Alice on the blower and a quick conversation before showtime. With the soundcheck over , I went outside to get some air and chill for a while. As I was slurping some coca cola this huge flying creature kept hanging around me freaking me out: like a wasp with an extra large body. I gave it a whack and as I did , this thing like a barb stuck in my hand. I pulled it out but the pain and swelling started immediately and soon , my hand was up to the size of a golf ball and numb in the process. I was running around like a headless chicken but Chryste sorted me out with some calming vibes and ointment , telling me it would be okay.

My sole concern was the gig and being able to drum okay. Would the swelling go down and the feeling return before the gig as I couldn't feel a fuckin' thing in my hand ?. After about an hour had elapsed , everything was back to normal and the show was an extremely sweaty affair for us all. Plenty of jokes about Ratty's hand dropping off and all the rest of it as we headed off to do one more

Holidays in the sun - Arizona

The walls were covered in western memorabilia old newspapers , six shooters and lengths of rope used by the goodies to actually hang the baddies with. Gruesome stuff as we stuffed ourselves to the limit before heading off to check out the famous OK Coral where Doc Holliday and Wyatt Earp took on the Clanton Gang. Our own Doc really enjoyed himself and had a few classic piccies taken with a dummy of Doc Holliday and we all bought Sheriff Of Tombstone badges before we saddled up and rode off into the sunset as all good cowboys do.

After leaving Arizona we headed off into Texas and Dallas with another monstrous journey to get through. Dallas was quite a shock : high rise buildings in abundance

Arizona show which was at Tucson where tumbleweed crossed our path and we had to keep our bins open for the Petrified Forest.

Had a right old laugh in that most western of western towns. Tombstone Arizona and the venue for the Gunfight At The OK Coral and the Boothill Cemetery. We stopped off at this wild west restaurant : I think it was called Waggon Wheel or something like that and had a storming nosh up.

and all looking very nice and clean but an uncomfortably high proportion of it is run down and full of ghettos and wastelands. We were down for The Institute and the guys who ran the club were complete fuckin' arseholes to say the least. They stuck us in a shithole of an excuse for a dressing room with an old rusty corrugated tin roof and the music in this hell hole was so fuckin' loud we couldn't hear ourselves speak as we tried to chill and prepare ourselves for showtime. The bass frequency was literally shaking the fuck out of the room but we hit the stage regardless of the shit going down around us. Throughout the show Nik gave out loads of shit to the audience and then all there was left to do was to pick up the pay cheque and skidaddle outta' there rapid after trashing the dressing room just to let the fuckers know we weren't happy with their shitty venue. We hated Texas and still had three shows to endure and all with the same boring fuckin' club owners who all had the same attitude of " Oh you are a rock band so we don't fuckin' like you guys ". Thick pricks !!

We hightailed outta' Texas as if we never saw it and journeyed back to the sunshine state of Florida to do four shows and all of them turned out to be fantastic affairs : plenty of spliffidge coke and other substances that helped us forget the banality of Texas. Our final night backstage saw us having a massive party which carried on back to the hotel along with all the people we'd invited back to share the remainder of the night with us. As we pulled up outside the hotel , the cops pulled us ; apparently following us for some time and there we were oblivious to them. This was indeed very bad news for us as we all had an awesome amount of gear on our persons.

Thoughts of being busted flashed into our minds as soon as we clocked the flashing blue light but Chryste played it ice cool throughout : walked over to the còp car and calmly explained that we were an English rock group who'd just finished a gig and were heading back to the hotel for a spot of understandable celebrations and awfully sorry for being a bit on the rowdy side. This cop couldn't believe his eyes when he saw our glorious leader : came over and told us all he remembered seeing us wayback in eighty two in none other than the Batcave. Originally from London, he was totally gobsmacked that here before his eyes were Alien Sex Fiend. Nik gave him a tee shirt and we all ended up having a right old snigger. Well pleased the incident had finished on a friendly note. The fuckin' cop a Fiend fan !!. Bizarre stuff.

Only a few dates left on the tour now and we took the same route back as our outward journey playing the same venues too ; ending up in New York at the Marquee where we bumped into Baron Puppet who'd done the first tour with us. Great to see the Baron again and we all had a good time re-establishing friendships with him. Poor old Baron had just been to the dentist for some serious root canal surgery and couldn't speak to save his life. The tour came to a thumping wig removing finale , signalling our exit from the Big Apple but not before we all sampled some of NY's finest pizzas. The

Nik and the cops !

same ones that made Joey Ramone what he was.

Sadly, it was that time again: goodbyes and best wishes to all the people who had worked so hard on the tour for us. Chryste , Beth and the two Sandras and all the other peeps who'd worked so hard in keeping things smooth. I'd had a brilliant time touring a country of such vast contrasting scenic and cultural differences , both good and bad. We'd put in thousands of miles on a punishing tour and we were all thoroughly fucked as we boarded the jet for the flight home. Mixed feelings of sadness and contentment filled me. Sad that such a fantastic experience had come to an end and content that I was finally heading home to family and friends.

The next year was to be one of such high and lows. Being financially stretched to my limits was a shit one to be in. I always made it my business to send cash home to Nicci whenever I was away with the Fiends but there was just never enough of the stuff to go round. I

faced a sad, frustrating irony that at times, tore me apart. On the one hand, being a member of a successful rock band travelling around the world playing to enthusiastic paying audiences, and yet, seeing hardly anything from it.

And on the other hand, a husband and father with a wife and child back home, relying on a regular income that was never there. This financial situation created massive problems for us. Eventually sewing the seeds of destruction of my marriage to Nicci.

Rat with Beth on the US tour bus

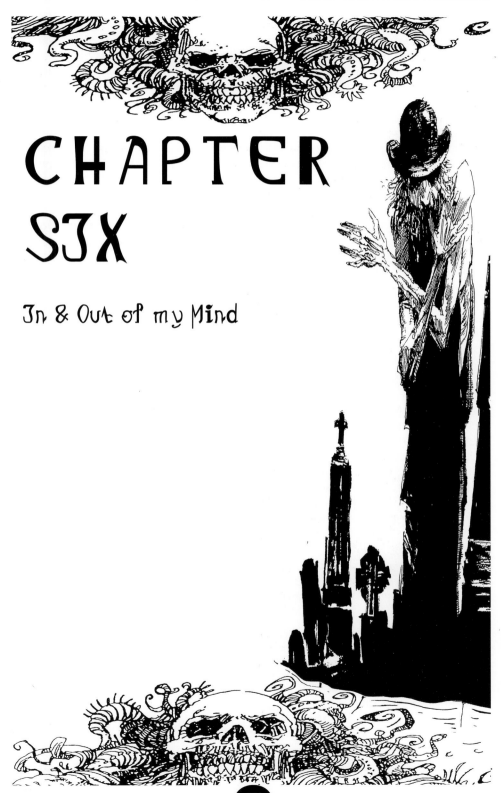

CHAPTER SIX

In & Out of my Mind

No time to think about anything though with the news that we were off on another German tour with a warm up gig at The Astoria. Despite being home with the people I loved, I was badly missing the buzz of touring so this was great news. Rehearsals were scheduled at The House In The Woods so it was wide smiles from yours truly : chunkier versions of Wild Women and Hee Haw came out of those sessions and ideas for a radical new stage set too from Nik. Stripped down with very little of the manic theatricals in evidence, apart from the mannequins and tubes all sprayed up in silver.

The London show was the bollocks and we opened up with I am A Product and then straight into Hee Haw as the Fiend fans went completely mental ; jumping off balconies and all the usual chaotic commotion. The new stage set looked fantastic with low floorlights, drum kit off centre and no risers : stripped down to the bare bone but still very effective visually. A reflection of Nik's ever changing artistic direction with regards to his mutant baby offspring. Everything was sorted for the German tour like never before. Shows all sold out well in advance and this tour bus with beds, television, video and an awesome sound system to keep the smiles on our faces. With the luxury of our own bunch of caterers to look after us, we all felt pretty special.

We arrived at Oberhausen, and a gig played out in a massive circus tent complete with huge PA system and all the other things needed for showtime. To the rear of the tent was a steel lions cage that served as a bar during the night ; pretty useful too if any drug induced deranged crazies got out of hand. The dressing rooms were caravans and the whole thing felt very travelling circus. What a fantastic gig Oberhausen turned out to be apart from the disappointment on Nik's face due to the fact he couldn't reach the trapeze to amaze us all with his gymnastic skills. On this tour we had Len dressed as the texas chainsaw murderer Ed Gein. He would appear just before showtime on stage and freak the shit out of the crowd. A nice little taster before we ripped 'em apart with our musical chainsaws.

Doc celebrated his birthday and in Lichtenfels, the two caterers Pinky and Perky sorted out an assortment of food, balloons and presents especially for the occasion. It was a total surprise to the Doctor and we all got severely brain damaged after the show. Back at the hotel Doc drank himself into another world ; mumbling away and blending into the wallpaper so well. After a sudden announcement that it was time for the bogs, we hear this almighty crash bang wallop and on investigation, find the Doctor heaped over the toilet with his noodle jammed into the basin. We finally sorted him out and got him to bed before crashing out ourselves.

The next bit of fun was at Biberach : the only place we didn't have a map to help us suss out exactly where the fuck we were going. To complicate matters even further, there are only six towns in Germany called Biberach and the obvious happened ; we arrived at the right Biberach and the equipment landed down at a completely different Biberach : result total fuck up !. Three hours later , amid a very friendly impromptu party the gear rolled into the right Biberach so we were sorted. Went on without a soundcheck and it all turned out okay in the end for us and the fans.

For the final show of the tour in Stuttgart , Pinky and Perky made us all a rather special goodbye chocolate spaceship cake full of dope that seriously lifted all our wigs off : real knock out cake ! There were loads of interviews to do that evening and all I could do was mumble a few sentences that must have sounded totally confusing: afterwards getting on the bus hallucinating and not recognising anybody around me. It was in that state that I said my goodbyes to Germany for one more time : heading back to Blighty before shooting off to Spain once again.

The Fiends were really cooking as a band at that point in time and we were all up and ready for just about anything that happened to come our way.

After the snow of Germany , the sun of Spain was most welcoming to me and I managed to find the time to check out the Salvador Dali Theatre Museum Figueres close to Barcelona. The place is crammed full of sculptures of all shapes and sizes : paintings in oil and watercolours everywhere. In the middle of the building is this open courtyard where people were busy shoving coins into a box by Dalis old Cadillac. Inside the car were these mannequins and loads of flowers and a grape vine that sprinkled water out everytime it

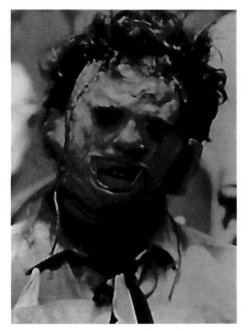

Leatherface himself from The Texas Chainsaw Massacre

received a coin , covering the inside of the car in artificial rain. What was he thinking about when he created that little lot I will never know but he is one of my constant inspirations through life.

We endured a hair raising journey across mountainous roads with sheer drops but we eventually reached Cadaques in one piece to check out the great mans house where he lived. It has these huge white eggs strapped to the walls and these weird looking elephants all over the place : you couldn't go into the house but I made up for that disappointment by actually sitting in exactly the same spot he'd sat in while painting the Persistence Of Memory. The one with the melting watch hanging on a tree and covered in ants.

The shows were excellent

and our hotel in Alicante was right on the beach looking out onto the sea : beautiful. I loved being in Spain because it's such a passionate place to live. Full of colour, vitality, diversity and beauty. The final show was top be at Mad Tonys ; one crazy fuckin' promoter. Talk about women and drugs ; he had both in abundance and well into the Fiends. He was so chuffed that we were finishing the tour in his club and gave him a show that turned out to be the usual very late Spanish affair for all concerned.

Cocaine and Mescal appeared in large amounts and we all ended up rocking in our coffins : played a mindblowing set that lasted some three hours in all : finally crawling out of Mad Tonys club around eight in the morning thoroughly fucked but needing to get our heads round the fact it was time to head back to Blighty. After arriving in Cardiff , Nik had to take the hire car back to the Hertz rental office so Doc and I followed in Nik's mini. As we hit Cardiff centre Doc fucked up on the gears ; stalled the car causing some bozo to run into the back of us but there was no damage. Nik sorted the geezer out in the other car while I calmed down the flapping Doctor.

I had loads of gifts for Nicci and Kashia and really enjoyed the time chilling out with my family after the madness of Germany and Spain. Kashia was growing up fast: changing all the time and we all had plenty of fun together. It was painful missing her development as a child but that's how it was. Money was the big nightmare and Nicci was forever on my case telling me I should be getting well paid for all

the hard work I was putting in with the Fiends but that was impossible.

Nik and Chris both made it crystal clear to me that there was no more money available : yes I could have gone to the musicians union but that would have been me finished with the Fiends. Nicci never let me forget that I was being totally abused by the Fiendish duo, but I had no choice but to live with it or be booted out. My loyalty to the band ensured I towed the financial line. The Doctor was in exactly the same position as I was so we just went along with it because the band was everything to us.

Fantastic news that a tour in Japan was about to break, but the domestic problems I faced with Nicci weighed me down badly The thought of leaving Nicci and Kashia with hardly any money to help them through while I was away touring was tearing me apart. I blew up several times : thought of kicking the Fiends into touch but it was Nicci's calm reassuring words that convinced me to follow my dream through to whatever conclusion it held for me. Nicci knew me inside and out and somehow, always gave me the strength to pick up my spirit when it was at it's lowest ebb." Ratty !. Just get out there and have a good time and don't you dare forget my Kimono ".

Japan was a serious culture shock in every way imaginable from the food to the size of baths : the flight lasting over fourteen hours and what a flight. This punk band from Blighty called Chaos were with us and appearing on the same bill so we all became chums despite them being a right load of nutters. Farting, getting pissed and generally annoying the delicate looking air hostesses who must have wondered what the fuck was going on. There are some things you do and definitely don't do on an airliner and they were doing everything you shouldn't.

We arrived in Tokyo at night; welcomed by an assortment of press and promoters and record company heads : whisked off to the venue for technical discussions and a very strange meal in between. All the gear was hired : brand spanking new and not a scratch on it and the drumkit I was given was awesome along with a wild lighting rig in the club and a feature that saw Benny having orgasms about.

We were then taken politely to our hotel after much bowing , handshaking and smiling, for a well earned wind down. The hotel served these weird looking drinks from this automatic drinks dispenser and one in particular called Pocari Sweat replaced the bodies lost salts and energy minutes after you'd managed to get it down your neck : one of the drinks I left out of my diet. Tokyo is like another planet : an alien world like something out of Bladerunner. Bright neon lights and pavement loudspeakers playing this trippy oriental music the whole time and beer and whisky available all day long from drinks machines dotted around the place.

In my hotel room next to the bed was this huge bouquet of flowers and loads of chocolates wishing me a most enjoyable stay and a successful tour in Japan. Nice friendly touch and a damm sight more than you get in UK hotels. I kipped in this really small bed and took a bath the following

morning in an even tinier bath : four foot long and three foot deep and very uncomfortable to lie in or rather crouch in. I had to hang my legs over the end so I could wash properly and all the time I was chuckling away at the thought of all the problems Moz would be having as he was well over six foot tall . Ah so !!

The first day was a meeting everybody concerned kinda day with loads of interviews , more bowing of heads , handshaking , smiling and all the other things we had to do while the crew were hard at work sorting out the gear for showtime : spraying up these odd looking dummies and all the dustbins ready to go on stage. The first gig was down for the Club Citta and we were told we could only do an hour so a lot of the songs were dropped. Doing Zombiefied was so funny with all these peeps stood there in front of us wondering what the fuck was going on while Nik's bouncing loads of skulls around the place ; booting them into the crowd as if he was knocking one in for his favourite team. " Come On You Hammers ".

The second night saw us straight into a faster paced set : this time they got the idea straight away and went fuckin' mental with loads of streamers going off all over the place. Balloons flying around and these noisy firecrackers banging in ya face. Afterwards backstage , the club owner apologised profusely for not having the sense to put us on at a bigger theatre venue in town but we didn't give a toss and reassured him we'd enjoyed ourselves immensely. Chaos were on the same bill : a real diehard hard core punk band who gave it

More Fiendish capers

loads whenever they played. The guitarist Gabba comes over drinking this stuff called Regain. Some crazy tonic drink with snake venom in it ; gave you a kick like a gramme of top quality charlie and they always had a fridge full of the stuff to keep 'em at it.

The next show up on the tour was at a place called Nagoya in this huge complex. The dressing room were really tiny affairs so we used the hotel to prepare ourselves for showtime. Top stars were to be found in the hotel during our residence there ; Tod Rundgren and Richard Clayderman. We finally took to the stage in a packed venue full of the most brilliant hairstyles I have ever come across. The Japanese take a great deal of pride in their appearance and did it show that night. The gig was a real shitkickin affair and we left 'em all for dead after Boneshaker Baby.

The bullet train is something else and everybody should travel on it once in their lives. It moves like lightning and all the time, waitress service to keep a smile on your face. We all tucked into what we thought were hot dogs only to discover that they were full of these noodles. Chaos were up to their usual fuckin' about tricks as soon as they sussed the seats swivelled round and you could face the person who was once sat behind you. If you aren't keen on them , simply swivel back and tuck into your noodle dog again without having to look at them.

We piled back to Tokyo after Nagoya and from my window I could see loads of little old ladies hard at work in the fields below : bent double and working the land and the whole thing reminded me very much of Apocalypse Now and the Killing Fields. It freaked me out for a time as you never see old ladies up to such things back in Blighty : made me think about my comfortable wild lifestyle and one I would not have relished swapping for all the Saki in Japan. It was a strange but very vibrant culture full of energy and by the end of it , it felt like our eyes were beginning to slant with the incessant bowing handshaking and smiling . Felt like we were actually turning Japanese I really think so !.

We finally reached our destination and took time out to shop and sightsee, visiting the Asakusa Temple and other such splendid buildings. Bought myself a load of toys , home made fans and of course , Nicci's Kimono ; couldn't forget that one ! We ate at a restaurant called Drastic ; luckily the food didn't reflect the name and we were served up with lots of fish dishes with plenty of rice wine to swill it all down with. Using chopsticks was hilarious and I could never get the hang of it. One of the smiling waiters took a shine to my tee shirt so after the meal , I obliged and gave it him before leaving the restaurant after a thoroughly enjoyable meal.

I would have loved to have seen so much more of the Japanese people and it's brilliant culture but sadly we didn't have the time. From the futuristic to the traditional and a revelation in every way. The way the Japanese have literally risen from the ashes of the nuclear holocaust to dominate the worlds market in so many products is a testament to their skills and I was really taking to the life when suddenly , we had to leave. So different compared to anywhere I'd ever visited. " ARRIGATO (THANKYOU) JAPAN !!

Home for Ratfink after Japan to chill with the family once again. Nicci had some fantastic news : the Pinewood Studios special effects boys were staging a horror exhibition, thanks to a great guy called Bob Keen of Image Animations. They were featuring original props and figures from classic films such as Hellraiser , Nightbreed , Alien and many others. Nicci and I went down to see if we could get involved with it in any capacity. Met the boss and told him I had just come off a tour with the Fiends and he went for it.

We were given the honour of standing outside the entrance to the exhibition in full horror gore make up, handing out leaflets and freaking all the heads out as they stolled up and down the prom sucking on toffee apples and ice cream. We met Martin Mercer and Paul Spatri ; both incredibly talented make up artists in their own right. Martin was totally gobsmacked when I told him I was in the Fiends and what a truly awesome make up job he did on the pair of us, and

proceeded to have a riot freaking out the straights as they stolled past wide eyed and open mouthed as soon as they clapped eyes on the pair of us. Had a chat with Nik and gave him the good news that the guys were prepared to do a number for us on the next Fiend video, and he was well pleased at their kind offer.

We bedded down in the studio to start recording material for a forthcoming new LP, coming up with loads of solid creative ideas for new tunes. Martin Mercer turned up with his magic pen and discussed the details for a new video to compliment the track called Magic ; a Fiendish little ditty containing loads of eastern promise. Nik and Martin decided to go for an Egyptian feel to the video with Mummies hands , rotting bandages , pyramids and all kind of tomblike props to enhance the footage.

We stayed in the studio for around seven weeks and put down some shitkickin songs in' that time. Class Of 69 and Coma were my two particular favourites of the lot. A very creative and positive time for my Fiend life but not so in my family life. I always remained in constant contact with Nicci throughout the lengthy recording session : flowers on her birthday and other things to let her know I loved and cared for her in my absences. But this time the vibes were all wrong when we talked down the telephone to one another. I had shitloads of studio stuff on my mind and because of this pressure , the situation was shelved until I could return home to sort it out personally. The studio was costing an arm and a leg and any emotional diversions from any of us would fuck things up so it was business first or else, under such circumstances as money wasn't exactly bulging inside our pockets.

I eventually arrived home to a flat in a terrible mess. Baby clothes, pots and pans everywhere. And then being told the shattering news from Nicci, she'd been having an affair with a seventeen year old boy. Told me she'd had it with my lifestyle : bored shitless of it and me being away all the time with very little to show for it when I came home. Money fuck up's once again, and it destroyed me even more when she told me the guy she was seeing came from a wealthy family and could treat her ; look after in a way I could only dream about.

All the touring and being away from home with nothing to show for it had split us apart. The damage was done. To help me cope with the bad news and the anger pulsing through me, I smashed my bedroom to pieces. Nicci took Kashia and left the home for a few days until I calmed down. A chance to look at the situation calmly and rationally, but I was in pieces and didn't know what to do about anything, so I kept my head low for a few days, trying to get a grip of the heartbreaking situation I found myself in.

Some semblance of normality returned and we both decided to put a brave face on it for Kashia's sake : Nicci returned back to the home and moved downstairs with the intention of keeping out of my way as much as possible. No physical contact whatsoever passed between us but we did have endless confusing conversations. Kashia didn't know what the hell was happening and neither did we. It all got the better of us and Nicci moved to a new flat with my daughter : a move that brought on the one hand, such a relief and yet, broke me up because we had finally split up.

I was at the lowest emotional time in my life : drastic action was called for to bring the spark back so it was off to the hairdressers and sort out a Sioux Indian style haircut with widows peak shaved into the front and all spiked up on top. " Feeling better already ". Next stop was the tattoo parlour and a four hour session of pain and magic ; Ratfink was reborn and ready to kick arse again despite the dreadful setbacks at home. The situation between Nicci and I eased somewhat and we often indulged in tea drinking sessions laced with heavy conversations about what was to be done. Liked my new appearance too and told me to be strong and stand on my own two feet more than ever , despite the break up. Sure it hurt both of us but it wasn't to be the be all and end all of everything.

Touring was upon me once again with a brand new LP called Open Head Surgery and with what I'd gone through over the recent weeks , a title I personally found very appropriate. Just before the tour kicked off for real , I headed down to Cardiff for the filming of this new promotional video Magic all done down at Franks club where we'd done some memorable shows in the past. Martin Mercer turned up with Martin Astles and together , they were responsible for some awesome looking props for the video.

The USA crew from the Open Head Surgery tour

tour bus to see the country in. Swarms of press and television appearances to promote the album and tour and once again , the vibe was electric within our little circle. Even one of the special effects guys ; Martin Astles decided he wanted in on the tour and throughout the shows he would appear on stage in this amazing Rat costume attacking us while at the same time , freaking the shit out of the audience with his antics.

This huge Egyptian style sarcophagus took centre stage that Nik was to lie in swathed in bandages and looking very Boris Karloff before rising from the dead in the finest Hammer Horror traditions. They'd even brought along a couple of the original corpses from Hellraiser and loads more Egyptian goodies to use. The shoot took some twenty four hours in all to complete and after it was done , we were all thoroughly knackered with heads crammed full of Egyptian vibes : all of us ready for some well earned zzzz's before the tour began.

For the new tour , we had a totally new stage set with lot's of projectors and none of the famous Sex Fiend muslin : a stripped to the bone set with Nik going through a change too : less hair and a drape coat looking for all the world like a decomposing Eddie Cochran. Doc Milton looking cool in his three piece suit and the delectable Mrs Fiend looking as good as ever. Germany was fantastic this time around in an even bigger and better

A short tour of Blighty followed before heading off for the States once again and what we hoped would be a major commercial breakthrough. I definitely thought that tour was the " this is it lads tour " as far as success goes and in many ways it was. Before leaving , we had a quick record store signing in London to get out of the way and took Martin along in his Rat costume to add another dimension to the event. He turned a few heads on the underground and was such a good laugh the whole time we knew him : up for anything anytime of the day or night.

That tour was our biggest and busiest and took Chryste some time to sort out all the business before we arrived on her doorstep. We played many crazy venues on that tour including Seattle ; the birthplace of grunge and a venue called The Rock Candy where many greats had appeared over the years. I remember being escorted from the stage after the show and on my way , this crazy girl jumped on top of me freaking me out . I tried to shake her off but she was having none of it : she had claws like a tiger and really dug her nails into my back , leaving me with some deep scratches right down my back and I was scarred for weeks after that gig ; crazy bitch : never got her number though but she left her mark on me in more ways than one. Ouch !!

Tulsa was a strange gig. I could never in my wildest dreams, have imagined I'd end up playing drums in Tulsa Oaklahoma in the United States Of America. It seemed the whole fuckin' town had turned out for this one and they really did look like a bunch of demented circus freaks. The venue was a tiny affair to say the least and the PA system was nearly as big as the one I had back home. The whole thing was just one great laugh from beginning to end and we said our goodbyes to Tulsa with more than a smile on our faces.

Being in LA the second time around was not as good as the first for me. We arrived there one month after the riots had taken place and the vibe was very scary indeed : we had to watch where we walked in case we ended up getting our heads blown off as there were a lot of angry gun toting people around still buzzing from the riots

and looking for the slightest excuse to pop off a few slugs. The gig was scheduled to take place in the South Central district : not one of safest areas LA has to offer the traveller but there you go. The ticket sales were disappointingly down compared to what we'd expected and the show was a mundane affair. A personal highlight being a shitkickin version of Zombified, and it was this version that featured on the live LP Altered States which was a result for us and the best thing to come out of that one.

While we were in Texas ; yeah that place again , we had some spare time to ourselves between gigs before heading off to Baton Rouge in Louisiana. The weather was stifling so this particular day , Benny and I decided on a spot of the old sunbathing by the hotel pool and what a pleasant time of things we had. Having a right old giggle chatting to a few nice girls ; one of which starred in an Alien Sex Fiend unofficial video if you know what I mean. This really friendly gorgeous blond girl just swam around the pool , diving and doing back flips and any other

More Fiendish action from the 1992 states tour

Coffee, spliff - sorted ! - relaxing Miami Beach style

couldn't get any shoes on my blistered feet. Later on throughout the whole of the tour , my skin peeled badly and I really thought I'd contracted some UV disease or something !. That fuckin' day in Texas I had my bacon well and truly fried !

flip you care to think of while the camera filmed her antics. We had a brilliant time with her and was definitely one of my Texan highlights. She was up for anything and soon things got silly : out came a big inflatable banana in the pool but to our regret she didn't have the pleasure of sampling any of our bananas that day.

That all day pool session caused Benny and myself so much agony. The sun was blistering and as a result of sitting out in it the whole day , both of us were lobstered to perfection. Really severe sunburn and I'm talking head to toe : so bad that Benny had to have a doctor to sort him out while I crashed down in bed. I couldn't move an inch it was that painful and even had to cancel some previously arranged jollities with a girl by the pool because of it.

The next day we set off for Baton Rouge and just about everybody did their fair share of taking the piss out of us. I had to do the gig with bare feet as I

We toured Florida once again and this time , I had the pleasure of getting to know a great babe called Stacia. Fiend mad she was and she insisted on staying with me until the end of the tour : well who was I to argue ?. She looked after me all the time and we both kept one another highly amused if you know what I mean. After years of being faithful to Nicci , it was high time to indulge in not only the drugs and the rock n roll but the sex bit of the triangle too and Stacia really did brighten up my touring days in Florida before we finally said our goodbyes to one another.

The tour came to another tearful ending with countless hugs, handshakes from everybody who'd worked their arses off in putting the Fiends together one more time. Getting home this time was not the pleasant experience it used to be : I was completely pissed off and missing Stacia around me so instead of sitting around and turning into a moody bastard , I booked a flight out to Florida and spent an unforgettable time with Stacia again, without the stress of rigorous timetables of touring to get in our way and we had an even better time of things than our first time round.

Sometime later, Nik and Chris received the news they were starting work on a brand new project called Inferno. A computer game they were asked to write all the music for : great I thought : a completely new galaxy for the crew of the Starship Sex Fiend to head off too but it seemed Nik and Chris had really gone for Inferno. Put all their eggs into one basket so to speak , while neglecting their original offspring they'd spent so much time looking after. Alien Sex Fiend as the band we and the fans knew and loved was hibernating. No more tours ; no new single we'd spent so much time discussing : nothing. . . . except this Inferno project.

The Fiendish duo based everything around themselves and Doc Milton and myself were left out on a limb with nothing to do except return to our lives before Alien Sex Fiend. Nik phoned me from time to time with general chit chat as well as going on about how exciting the new project was for them but something that didn't interest me in the slightest. I wanted in on the Fiends again but as they were : full of attitude and in ya face music : nothing less. It pissed me off badly, because we all had that vibe within the band that the next thing to come out was going to be the one to put us on the map but it just wasn't to be. One of those feelings I mentioned that you have just gotta' go with but one this time , we didn't go with. It just didn't happen the way I wanted it to happen ; the way I'd dreamed it happening so many times.

CHAPTER SEVEN

R.I.P.

Who are you calling nosey !

That was it. My life with Alien Sex Fiend had ended : confirmed in a telephone call from some Fiend fans telling to me they'd received the latest Fiend info sheet from Nik and Chrisì, that I was no longer in the band. The guitaring had gone to a guy called Dave Dearnley and Doc Milton had apparently quit to pursue his recording studio work.

A simple message. . . . " To go where my sticks would take me ! ". . . .a comfortable way for Nik to tell the fans I'd moved on but to me, anything but comfortable. The news totally fucked me off. After giving my heart and soul to the band for eight years, and not being told face to face that I'd been sacked. I was well and truly redundant both musically and spiritually. Detached from all the great memories shared along the way. The lid on my coffin was well and truly nailed shut by the man I

never for one second imagined, would personally hammer the nails in.

He laid this big moral speech on me one time about loyalty and devotion. Both of us seriously stoned with Nik getting deep into me with this threatening manner he had about him whenever he thought he was being ripped off or whatever. Told me that if I ever left the band, wanting to do my own thing and didn't let him know the score, then he would take great delight in pushing me down the ladder because nobody ever get's one over on old Nik. And there he was preaching a totally different gospel to the one he read to me that night. Done in a sneaky, calculating cloud of ambiguity with his well chosen words. . . ." Ratty will go wherever his sticks will take him ". . .yeah right ! It still pisses me off that someone so upfront, confident, had to resort to the easy way to get rid of me.

Looking back to those mad crazy times, most of my time was spent living under the threat of the sack. Often, Nik would go into one, scaring the shit out of us all with his fits of manic rage whenever things happened to go wrong. He knew the band was my life. I mean it cost me everything for fucks sake, my marriage included, but despite all the shit, I adopted a policy of appeasement to keep in there. At times, it became very awkward to put forward any suggestions of enhancing the band ; trying to make it more commercial so we could pull in all the luxuries you normally associate from a rock and roll lifestyle.

He always saw great

potential in everything he created and was up for pushing it further than perhaps, the great showman himself intended his baby to go. I don't know the reasons behind this but maybe, Nik was a little scared of the monster he'd created and didn't want it to grow the way I wanted it too. After all, the band was very much Nik and Chris's little baby and they made sure it was never overfed with anything but their own ideas and input. It was as if he was blind to the brilliance of the package he'd put together in Alien Sex Fiend and wanted it to go no further than cottage industry, whereas I wanted to go PLC with branches worldwide.

I still hold the greatest respect for Nik Fiend. He was one of the funniest, charismatic, artistic, visually creative people to walk the planet

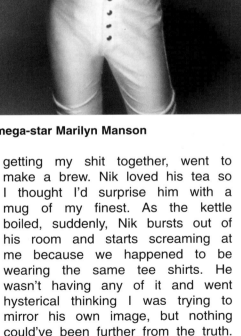

Goth rock mega-star Marilyn Manson

but on the other hand, when he became confused, he would explode ; literally biting the head off anybody who got in his way. Including the people who loved and cared for him, and I do include myself in those people, despite the ending. Many times it came down to a simple, basic equation : behave or fuck off !

We'd arrived back from Scotland one time, chilling out in the big house in Cardiff. All the crew and band were presented with these tasty tee shirts, and after

getting my shit together, went to make a brew. Nik loved his tea so I thought I'd surprise him with a mug of my finest. As the kettle boiled, suddenly, Nik bursts out of his room and starts screaming at me because we happened to be wearing the same tee shirts. He wasn't having any of it and went hysterical thinking I was trying to mirror his own image, but nothing could've been further from the truth.

As I backed off down the stairs, he came at me ; seriously threatening to punch the fuck out of me and all for nothing. It was all becoming very edgy and so many times, Nik spat his venom on the people who cared for him, whenever the dark clouds surrounded him. Talk about blowing hot and cold. Nik wrote the book on it and at times, was his own worst enemy. The likeable, infectious joker one second: the screaming Tasmanian Devil the next !

With the Fiend empire being very much a family run concern, the other band members were constantly kept in the background in case they attracted recognition. In the eight years I played with them, I find it pretty amazing that I never once received fan mail from anybody. Not even something saying " I saw you in Milton Keynes. You are a big headed fucker. Now fuck off and die ! ". There was nothing. Considering we had such a fiercely loyal army of fans unafraid of voicing their opinions, I find the whole thing bizarre.

The androgynous Manson

So now you know, anybody out there who took the trouble to pen me a few lines and never received a reply. My sincere apologies but the mail never reached me. It's only now, looking back in retrospect, I can see

Marilyn Manson and band

everything for what it was. I was far too concerned with keeping my place in the band. I showed a total unswerving blind loyalty to Nik to make sure I never missed out on a single second of being a Fiend. That was what mattered to me : consequently I took all the shit he gave out, even though at times, it was hard to swallow but swallow it I did.

And the countless times Nik manipulated us with joints to get us round to his way of thinking and doing. If ever I disagreed, then it was time for a joint. All the time, I felt like he was keeping me under wraps in case the limelight suddenly switched from him to me. I lived and breathed the Fiends and as far as I was concerned, any contribution both visually and musically I could make was done for the good of the band ; no other Like the time Nik and Chris were due to appear on television to promote the computer game they were developing. I took this as a golden opportunity to revive a flagging career as the show was going out to around seven million kids. I'm looking the bollocks : new shiny PVC trousers and hair looking mean and moody. As we left make up, Nik turns round and screams. . ." Ratty !! What the fuck are you doing wearing PVC trousers. Go and stick your jeans on cause they look better ". I just couldn't get through to him anytime, that everything I did was done to enhance the bands image as a band, and not for stupid selfish gain.

I never once felt the need to step on Nik's boots. I mean we were a band for fuck sake and not

your average band so why not go out looking the business everytime ? We were Alien Sex Fiend building up an awesome reputation for great live shows so why not shock to rock ? It felt we were all in competition with Nik and that nobody was going to steal his show. Take Doc Milton for example, sacked the same way I was. The Fiendish duo told the fans he'd gone off to work with various bands but no mention of the bands he was working with.

Bands like Big Country, Souxsie and the Banshees, Carter USM, Manic Street Preachers, to name but a few. What they put out in the fanzine was a gross understatement to Doc Miltons talents and the fans wouldn't have been aware that he was in fact, held in such high regard by those who worked with him. And neither would they have known anything about the way both of us were conveniently swept under the carpet, but now I can set the record straight for both Doc and myself.

Marilyn Manson is reaping in the kind of success I hoped the Fiends would. I felt strongly that the next material to be released after the Open Head Surgery tour would have catapulted us all into the world where Manson are wallowing. We were ready for it after all the tours ; after working our arses off to get that wealth and success that rock and roll bestows on it's subjects. I wanted the pad with the swimming pool in Beverley Hills, the speedboat, the cars : I wanted the world but Nik didn't have the vision or ambition to go further. In many ways, I liken him to the guy struggling to sell shoes on a freezing cold market stall. Doing alright if you know what I mean, but not good enough to go high street! A great shame.

Manson have got the financial backing to allow them to fully experiment in all the areas I wanted the Fiends to delve in. Since Nirvana and the death of grunge, there has been no significant musical statement to get the kids up and at it. I strongly approve of Manson. His twisted androgynous devil worshipping alter ego creates hate in people, and people need to hate something. Alice did it brilliantly : Rotten put the icing on the cake and now, Manson are shaking up the establishment ; encapsulating everything with their powerful, grinding, dirty filtered music combined with tricky intelligent videos. Blood, gore, horror, sexual schizophrenia : they have it all, just as Alien Sex Fiend had it when we stalked the stage.

It truly saddens me the Fiends didn't get to those places other bands these days are at. It wasn't to be, and now, will never be. Alien Sex Fiend are still alive, but gone the manic theatricals and powerful sounds : replaced with a format that has nothing to do with what they originally stood for and gave out. I had a fantastic time with Alien Sex Fiend. You never know where you can end up when a guy you've never met before, arrives to whisk you off down the motorway to begin living a dream you always dreamed of living.

But what's done is done ! And life goes on for me. Nicci and I are still very close and will forever be so. She takes the greatest care of my daughter Kashia, who I now see more than ever at a time, I'm feeling comfortable in life, both in myself and surroundings. Rooted and less nomadic, thanks to a number of creative media and musical projects I'm developing. I'm enjoying life these days and who knows. Maybe at some point in time, Kashia will grasp the chance to live out her own dreams. For her sake, I hope so.

THE FIENDISH
SCRAPBOOK

Ratty's new jungle rock band
- the one and only Uncle
Fester

Smile please !

Ratty in major
goth' mode...

The German crew of 89 (from left to right) :-
Michael Loffler and kikk (Hammer Promotions),
Benny, Nik, Chris, Doc, Rat, Wolfgang, Andy
Roberts

Nobody likes me.. but we adore you -
Edinburgh 1989

In the studio recording Here
Cum Germs in '8z

Nik boasting again !

Ratty struts his axe-hero stuff in Brighton '92

Miami beach from the fiends' hotel window - '89 tour

Hammer Films seminal Dracula - a prime
influence on Ratty

The eyes have it !

Count Dracula - Christopher Lee

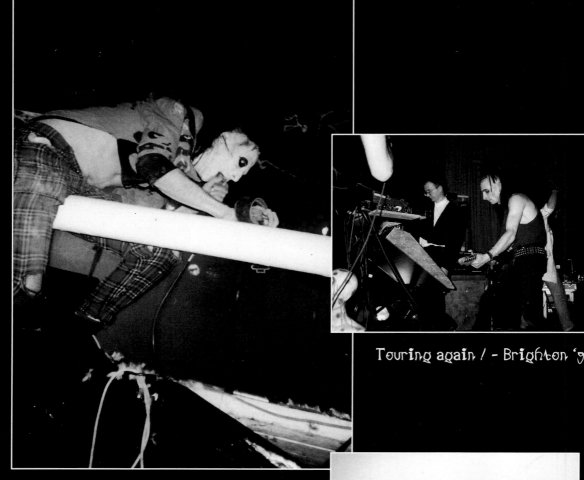

Touring again / - Brighton '9

Next stop is the drain / - Yugoslavia
Festival '90

Only the blind follow me
- video shoot for Ignore

Reflecting memories ...

Smells like..... Cardiff ///

t & Nik - The Droogies !!

5.30am & wasted in the stud
recording Here Cum Germs

Mr Demon in Berlin !

Alien Sex Fiend back catalogue releases are all available from :-

Cherry Red Records
Unit 17
1st Floor
Elysium Gate West
126/128 New King's Road
London
SW6 4LZ

Mail Order hotline : (tel) 0207 371 5844 (fax) 0207 384 1854

e-mail: infonet@cherryred.co.uk
www. cherryred.co.uk

Alien Sex Fiend back catalogue videos are available from:-

Visionary
2nd Floor
St Anne's House
329 Clifton Drive South
Lytham St Anne's
FY8 1LP

(tel) 01253 712453 (fax) 01253 712362

e-mail: nicky@visionary.co.uk
www. state51.co.uk/state51/visionary/

Noir Publishing
Mail Order Sales:
PO Box 28, Hereford HR1 1YT
e-mail: noir@appleonline.net

Noir books should be available from all good bookstores;
please ask your local retailer to order from:

UK & EUROPE:
Turnaround Publisher Services
Unit 3
Olympia Trading Estate
Coburg Road
Wood Green
London
N22 6TZ
Tel: 0181 8293000 Fax: 0181 881 5088

USA:
LPC Group
1436 West Randolph Street
Chicago
Illinois 60607
Tel: 312 432 7650 Fax: 312 432 7603

Canada:
Marginal Distribution
Unit 102
277 George Street
N.Peterborough
Ontario
K9J 3G9

Other titles available from Noir Publishing :-

Necronomicon Book Three
The Dead Walk